Access 2000
An Advanced Course for Students

Access 2000
An Advanced Course for Students

Sue Coles
Department of Business and Management Studies
Crewe and Alsager Faculty
Manchester Metropolitan University

Jenny Rowley
School of Management and Social Sciences
Edge Hill College of Higher Education

Learning Matters

First published in 2000 by Learning Matters Ltd.
Reprinted in 2001.

British Library Cataloguing in Publication Data
A CIP record for this book is available from the British Library.

ISBN 1 903300 15 0

Cover and text design by Code 5 Design Associates Ltd
Project management by Deer Park Productions
Typeset by PDQ Typesetting
Printed and bound in Great Britain by The Baskerville Press Ltd, Salisbury, Wiltshire.

Learning Matters Ltd
58 Wonford Road
Exeter EX2 4LQ
Tel: 01392 215560
Email: info@learningmatters.co.uk
www.learningmatters.co.uk

Contents

Other titles in this series

This is one of a series of course books for students, covering the three major components of the Microsoft Office 2000 suite of software.

Access 2000
An Introductory Course for Students
Sue Coles and Jenny Rowley
ISBN 1 903300 14 2

Access 2000
An Advanced Course for Students
Sue Coles and Jenny Rowley
ISBN 1 903300 15 0

Excel 2000
An Introductory Course for Students
Jim Muir
ISBN 1 903300 16 9

Excel 2000
An Advanced Course for Students
Jim Muir
ISBN 1 903300 17 7

Word 2000
An Introductory Course for Students
Sue Coles and Jenny Rowley
ISBN 1 903300 18 5

Word 2000
An Advanced Course for Students
Sue Coles and Jenny Rowley
ISBN 1 903300 19 3

To order, please contact our distributors:
Plymbridge Distributors, Estover Road, Plymouth, PL6 7PY.
Tel: 01752 202301   Fax: 01752 202333   Email: orders@plymbridge.com

Learning with this book

This book introduces Access 2000, the latest version of Microsoft's Access database management software. Access provides a range of features for database creation, storage and retrieval. In addition, professional on-screen forms and reports are easily designed using a range of colours and fonts. Access is a component of the Office2000 suite of application software, which also includes Word, Excel and PowerPoint. Data can be easily transferred between these different applications.

The book is designed for anyone who wants to learn how to use Access. This includes students in further and higher education, and professional users who need to develop small database applications and gain a familiarity with practical database concepts. Students who might benefit from this book are likely to be studying databases as part of an information systems, information management, business studies, management studies, or marketing course.

Approach

The underlying philosophy of this book is concerned with learning by doing. Readers should not only learn how to create a database application by working through this book, but they should also develop a conceptual framework around the issue of the use and design of databases that should help them to understand and design database applications using other software, and in a host of different application areas.

The unique and popular feature of the book is the focus on tasks and activities. Each topic gives you a number of exercises to complete. In each topic, the relevance and function of the new concepts are explained, and detailed instructions are given on how to carry out the exercises. As you work through the book you will gradually build up a database application for Total Health and Fitness, a fictitious sports and fitness activities facility. Later exercises use tables, forms, queries and reports that you have created earlier in the book, so that instead of re-working basic operations you are continually refining your application.

The book can be used as a basis for independent study or as the basis for class activities. In either context it is important to:
- Work methodically through the exercises in the order in which they are presented; data entered in earlier exercises is frequently re-used in later exercises.
- Take time for rest and reflection and break learning into manageable sessions.
- Think about what you are doing!
- Expect to make mistakes; think about the consequences of mistakes and learn from them. If you never make a mistake you will not learn as much from this book as someone who has had to experiment and deviate from the instructions.
- Remember that this book hasn't got all of the answers. It is selective. Continue learning by experimentation, and by using help and other guides after you have mastered the content of this book.

This title is an advanced course on Access 2000. If you find this text too challenging, we recommend that you use the slower paced version *Access 2000: An Introductory Course for Students*. Both books start with the basics, so it is perfectly possible for novices who are prepared to accept the challenge of this book to start with it. The approach does not assume any previous knowledge of databases.

Features in the text

The following features have been used throughout the book to make the practical instructions clear:

1. Bold capitals indicate a feature from the screen, for example **BUTTON** or **DIALOG BOX NAME**.
   Menu instructions are also presented this way: **EDIT-COPY** means choose **COPY** from the **EDIT** menu.

2. White bold capitals in a panel indicate the names of keys on the keyboard, for example **ESC** or **F1**.

3. Bold text in upper and lower case indicates names of **Fields**, **Tables**, **Queries**, **Forms** and **Reports**.

4. Italic text on a shaded background indicates *Text to be keyed in*.

Getting acquainted with Access

Topic objectives

This topic will show you how to:

- understand the definition and use of databases
- understand the Access window and the database window
- use help and the Office Assistant
- be aware of the components of an Access database application.

What is a database?

A database is a structured collection of related data. While not all databases are in electronic form, today most are and so it is electronic databases that are the theme of this book. All organisations collect data, and use this to keep records of the transactions they perform with suppliers and customers. Large database applications have been common in industry for many years. Databases of parts are important in production and maintenance applications in the engineering industry. Service-based industries, such as the health service or the banking industry, are particularly interested in databases of customers or clients. Each department or function within a business maintains a database that supports its specific activities. Thus finance departments have large databases that allow them to record the financial transactions that have been undertaken in the business, ranging from payment of salaries to sales and purchases. Marketing departments will maintain databases that show sales orders placed, the performance of specific sales staff and customer profiles. Earlier databases tended, largely, to be text and number based but now images, pictures, video clips and sound may be embedded in multimedia database applications.

Typically, a database holds data in the form of records. Each record relates to one transaction (e.g. a sales order) or one item or individual (e.g. a patient). Any specific database has a standard record format, and the same details are stored in each record. So, for example, if the database stores the name, address, age and sex of one customer, it will generally store the same data for each other customer whose details have been entered on the database. You may find it useful to look at the data in the Appendix as an example of the type of data that can be stored in a database.

The Appendix shows several sets of data. Most database applications involve a number of linked tables. Accordingly, as we develop the application in this book (a database for Total Health and Fitness), you will need to create a number of tables. We discuss the approaches to linking tables together more fully in Topic 22. Linking tables means data can be drawn from more than one table to support the creation of a subset of all the data held in the database.

When data is stored in a computer, software is needed to present that data to us – as users – in a form we can work with. If we want to add to, edit or retrieve the data then the software must be able to translate our commands into a form the computer can use. This kind of software is known as a database management system (DBMS) and Access is one of the most powerful industry-standard DBMSs that runs on a personal computer.

The Access window

When you first start Access, by double-clicking on its icon and choosing **START USING ACCESS**, the Access window shown in Figure 1.1 is displayed. Here you may choose whether to create a new database or open an existing one. The background window is inactive but notice it has the following components:

- **TITLE BAR** – shows you are in Microsoft Access.
- **ACCESS CONTROL MENU** – in the very top left-hand corner.
- **ACCESS MAIN MENU** – showing the menus.
- **TOOLBAR** – most icons are not available as the **MICROSOFT ACCESS** dialog box is active.
- **STATUS BAR** – at the bottom of the screen. Indicates status, e.g. 'Ready'.

2

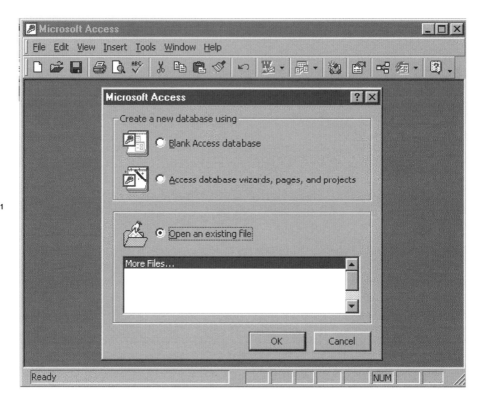

FIGURE 1.1

The database window

Once you have created (you will see how to do this in Topic 3) or opened a database, a window like the one in Figure 1.2 is displayed. This window allows you to create or access any object (table, query, form, report, etc.) in the database by clicking on one of the objects in the **OBJECT** list on the left side of the window. Initially, the **TABLES** object is selected and a window displays all tables in the database. If the window contains 'Create table' options only, as illustrated, then no tables have been created.

FIGURE 1.2

3

When the Database window is open, the Access window has the following components:

- **TITLE BAR**, which shows the Control menu icon (the key), the name of the application, and the window-sizing buttons.
- **DATABASE WINDOW MAIN MENU** showing the **FILE**, **EDIT**, **VIEW**, **INSERT**, **TOOLS**, **WINDOW** and **HELP** pull-down menus.
- **TOOLBAR** with only two active buttons, for either starting another new database or for opening an existing one. Note that all toolbar options have equivalent menu selections.

The Database window has the following components:

- **TITLE BAR**, which shows the Control menu icon (three documents), the name of the database and the window-sizing buttons. Note that if you do not specify a name for your database then Access will give it the name **db1**.
- **TOOLBAR** which allows you to create a new object, open an existing object or open an existing object in Design view.
- **OBJECT LIST**, which allows you to choose which type of object you want to work with.
- **MAIN WINDOW AREA**. This lists all the objects of the type selected in the Object list. When you create tables, queries, forms and reports you will give them names to identify them and these will be listed here.

■ **STATUS BAR**. Messages are displayed on the left of the status bar, for example, **Ready**. Modes are displayed on the right. For example, **NUM** indicates the number section of the keyboard is in number rather than cursor control mode.

What is an Access database?

Access is a database management system and it provides a means of storing and managing data or information. Microsoft refers to Access as a 'relational database product' since it allows you to relate data from several different sets or tables. This concept will be considered in Topic 22.

There are four main components of (or *objects* in) an Access database. These are:

■ tables
■ queries
■ reports
■ screen forms.

Tables

Access stores data in tables that are organised by rows and columns. The basic requirement of having a database is that you have at least one table. The columns in the table represent specific details (for example, the selling price of a property). The rows contain the collection of specific details and are known as records. Records are discussed in more detail in Topic 2.

Queries

A query is a question. There isn't a lot of point in storing data if you can't ask questions of it. For example: what is Dave Green's telephone number? How many sales were made in the south-east region during the last quarter? How many houses in a particular district are for sale? Queries are used to select records from a database to answer such questions. This type of query is known as a *select* query and, although Access provides other types of query, it is the one most commonly used.

Reports

Reports are used to print information. This may be based on all the data, in which case the report takes its input from a table, or it may be based on a selection of data, in which case the report takes its input from a query. Reports, therefore, can show the data from either a table or a query. In addition to data from records, they may show summary information relating to the data in the records displayed.

Screen forms

Screen forms are used to customise the way in which the data from records in tables or queries is displayed on screen. Their main purpose is to provide a user-friendly interface for the entry of new records or for the editing existing records.

Text can be added to a form to act as labels and instructions to the person entering the data. The appearance of text on a form can be changed by changing the font or by adding bold or italic emphasis. Text can also be shown as raised or sunken or displayed in a specific colour, and lines and rectangles can be added to give the form a pleasing appearance.

To emphasise the distinction between reports and forms: reports are intended to be printed; screen forms are normally displayed on screen, although facilities often exist for printing them.

Most applications will have a few screen forms for data entry and a larger number of standard reports. These reports can be created by using and arranging subsets of the same information. For example, a mailing list of clients may simply show customer name and address, but a list showing outstanding orders to a specific client will also show details of the items customers have ordered, their value and other associated information.

Components of databases

Answer the following questions:

1 What components of a database can a report be based upon?

2 What is a 'select' query?

3 What is a table? Why is it the most important component of a database?

4 What is a screen form?

Help and the Office Assistant

There are several main methods of getting into the help system. You only need to use one of these:

- Pull down the **HELP** menu and select **MICROSOFT ACCESS HELP.**
- Press the function key **F1.**
- Click on the **OFFICE ASSISTANT** ⬚. button on the toolbar. The Office Assistant dialog box will pop up with a choice of topics related to what you are currently doing as well a request box into which you can type a question.
- Pull down the **HELP** menu and select **WHAT'S THIS** or press **SHIFT + F1**. The pointer changes, with a question mark after it, and it can be used to point to anything. Clicking on that object will then bring up help. For instance, in this way you may get help on the meaning of all the items in the status bar. To remove the question mark, press **ESC**.
- In most dialog boxes there is a help button. This has a ? (question mark) on it, on the title bar. Click on this and then click on the part of the dialog box you want more information about.

Working with toolbars, menu bars and shortcut menus

If you are new to Office 2000 you may be unfamiliar with the approach Microsoft has adopted for toolbars, menu bars and shortcut menus. To find out more about these click on the Office Assistant and key in the question *working with menus*. Click on **SEARCH** and then select **WORK WITH TOOLBARS** and then start by choosing **READ ABOUT TOOLBARS, MENU BARS AND SHORTCUT MENUS**.

Tables, records and fields

Topic objectives

The exercises in this book create a database for Total Health and Fitness, a private fitness and sporting facility. In this book you are given a set of tables, reports and forms to create part of the information system Total Health and Fitness might find useful in running their business. Because the primary focus of this book is to introduce Access, we have relieved you of the need to think too carefully about the nature of the data and the way it is structured in the databases. In other words, we have done the database design for you. In order, however, that you appreciate some aspects of database design and understand why you are performing the tasks in this book, this topic introduces a few key aspects of database design.

This topic will show you how to:

- appreciate the need to analyse data before creating a database
- understand that, within a database, data is kept in tables and that there may be more than one table in a database, and that these tables can be linked together
- know that tables are composed of records which in turn are composed of fields
- be aware of the different data types available with Access.

Database design

We introduced the concept of a table, and its related reports, forms and queries, in Topic 1. There are two important questions for all database designers:

1. How do we decide what information or data to store in a database?

2. How should we structure that data?

The process that answers these questions is generally described as 'systems analysis', and there are many different approaches or methods that inform the way in which organisations ask themselves these questions in order that they can eventually arrive at a useful database. Many of these methods are designed to accommodate the complex systems that are used by many people and that are characteristic of large organisations. However complex (or simple) the system, there is one way to answer the fundamental question, and that is to ask:

1. What data do we require out of the system?

2. In what format will that data be most useful?

Accordingly, database design starts with outputs or an analysis of the data the organisation needs to support its activities. Since most businesses have a wide range of activities, information systems and the databases at the heart of these systems cover a wide variety of different functions in the organisation. Information systems may support ordering, personnel functions, management, production, sales, finance and marketing. In early systems, each of these different areas of activity within an organisation was supported by different systems but, with the advent of DBMSs integrated systems have become the norm. One of the important values of such integrated systems is that all parts of an organisation can share the same data and can use this as a basis for creating a shared knowledge base.

The database application for Total Health and Fitness has been chosen because we think it is important you have some appreciation of how the database application you are creating relates to the activities of a hypothetical organisation. We believe a health and fitness centre offers a simulated model that should be reasonably accessible to our readers.

The Appendix summarises the data you will use in the creation of the application. In the early topics we shall focus mainly on the **Client** table. For a membership-based organisation, such as Total Health and Fitness, it is important to know who the clients are. Should they also want to customise their letters, marketing communication or services, it is useful to have other data about their clients in addition to contact details (such as their interests and occupation). The precise data they have decided to keep in this table depends both on what data they are likely to need and also the way in which they are likely to use it. Total Health and Fitness didn't just dream up a set of data to collect. They asked themselves what reports or outputs they are likely to need to produce. In Topics 14–17, we create a number of different reports. The first report created in Topic 14 simply lists all of the data that we have on all members in the database. Whilst this is an interesting first exercise, Total Health and Fitness are unlikely to use this report very often because it uses too much paper (if you have 3000 members!) and it doesn't give any ready profile of the membership. The next report is a summary report, showing much less detail for each member but organising the list by client status number. This might be more useful for viewing the names and numbers of people in each category. In Topic 16 we create mailing label reports, which simply print name and address on to a label (provided you put labels in the printer!). To return to the key point: most organisations are seeking a wide range of different outputs from a database. Understanding these outputs and their relationship to the organisations' activities is the first stage of database design.

The next stage of database design is the identification of the data elements (e.g. date of birth, town, name) that should be stored in the database and the way in which these data elements should be structured into tables. Again, the Appendix shows several tables for the Total Health and Fitness database. These include a table that shows the sessions in which clients can participate, and the reservations table that records the classes for which an individual member has made a prior reservation. The database designer needs to decide whether the data relating to the location of a class goes in the sessions table or the reservations table. Data will be analysed into tables using processes such as entity relationship analysis and normalisation. At a pragmatic level, it is probably sufficient to think in terms of a key data element, or entity (thing), and to create a table around it by collecting other data elements that are intimately related to it (normally described as its attributes). You should be able to see how this has been achieved in the tables in the Appendix.

Finally, in this section, it is important to emphasise that the database application created in this book is only part of the database system Total Health and Fitness might find useful. In addition it is greatly simplified. For example, the application does not accommodate the record-keeping associated with alternative methods of payment, such as direct debit and annual subscription. Also, similar organisations, such as all estate agents or all publishers, need similar database applications. There is a range of specialist database software in the marketplace to meet the needs of such categories of organisations. Such applications usually provide a framework within which an organisation can configure the system to meet its specific requirements. Even organisations in the same industry or sector do not have identifiable systems needs and database applications.

Records and fields

As discussed above, a table generally holds data about one type of thing, for example, members of Total Health and Fitness. There are usually lots of this particular thing (say, tens or hundreds of different members). A table has the capacity to hold the same data about each of the occurrences of the entity. So a table of data about members of a sport and fitness centre would hold a standard set of details about each member. This set of details about each individual occurrence (such as an individual member) is known as a *record*. For each member there is a separate record in the table. Each record is composed of data about the member (such as name, address and so on).

Each piece of data within the record is known as a *field*. As you progress through the topics you will see how each field in a record needs to be defined before data can be entered into the record. Fields are given names to describe the kind of data they will eventually hold. It is important to distinguish between the *name* of a field and the *data* that field contains. For example, the field named **Last Name** will hold people's last names, such as 'Harris'. The field names can be considered to be the column headings in the table and each row in the table is a separate record. Therefore, each record in the table will have fields with the same name but containing different data. The records are displayed in this form in the datasheet but, if we use forms or reports, we can format the data in a wide variety of different ways. It is not always necessary to show all the data for a record, or all the records. In this way it is possible to select parts of a database for certain purposes and also to define who (within or outside an organisation) can see what records and fields. So, for example, Total Health and Fitness might use a swipe card entry system. This system will use the client number embedded in the swipe card bar code to identify the client. It will access the date of the last renewal field in the clients table and calculate whether the client has a current subscription. On the basis of this calculation it will flash up one of two messages: **CLIENT OK** or, **PLEASE REMIND THE CLIENT THAT THEIR SUBSCRIPTION IS OVERDUE**.

The way in which data is structured into the field is determined by the way in which it is to be used. So, for example, why have we split the name in the **Client** table into last name, first name and title? We could just have used one field, called name. This split allows the use of any of the components separately. So if, for example, we want to address a personalised letter 'Dear Joe', with a separate first name field, we can pull this out on its own. We might then go on to address the envelope for the letter: 'Mr Evans'.

It is important that each record is different from every other record so it can be selected without confusion. If more than one person has the same last name, some other field needs to be considered to differentiate between the records (for example, first name). An identifying field such as a number (say, employee number), is often created to make it easier to make each record unique. This field can be used as a primary key. A *primary key* is a field (or combination of fields) that uniquely identifies a record. In the **Client** table, **Client No** is used as this primary key whilst, in the **Session** table, **Session No** is used as such a key.

Data types

Table definition is the first step in building the database – that is, giving the table a name and defining the names of the fields that will be contained in each record in the table.

The next step is to define type of data to be stored in each of the fields. Before data can be entered into a database the nature of each of the field needs to be defined. Take the member's last name. First, the field name needs to be specified (i.e. Last Name). Next, it is necessary to indicate whether the data is text, numeric or date/time.

Every field in your table will be of a particular data type (for example, a name is alphanumeric text, a price would be currency and a date would have a date data type). The data type you choose for your field determines the kind and range of values that can be entered into it and the amount of storage space available in the field. Select the appropriate data type for each field. For example, you will probably define most fields in a table of names and addresses as text fields.

Sometimes a text field should be used when the data is numbers. Fields such as telephone numbers, or bank account numbers that contain digits only should be defined as text fields. The reason for this is that there is no need to do calculations with telephone numbers or bank account numbers. Often telephone area codes start with a zero, which is not allowed in a true number. Account numbers may also start with one or more zeros (known as *leading zeros*). So, reserve the number data type for fields on which you want to perform calculations.

The following data types are some of the key ones available in Access:

- *Text*: Text and numbers. By default Access will make a text field 50 alphanumeric characters long. This means you can enter data (letters and numbers) up to this length. If you know the length of the longest piece of data to be entered into the field, you can specify this as anything from 1 to 255 characters. Examples of text type fields are names and addresses and session activity.
- *Number:* Numerical data on which you intend to perform mathematical calculations (except calculations involving money or dates). You will see later that there are different number data types, which define the size of number you wish to store and whether the data is whole numbers or decimal numbers. A typical numeric field would be number of items in stock.
- *Auto Number:* Sequential whole numbers automatically inserted by Access so you do not need to enter the data into the field. Numbering begins with 1 and increases by 1 each time data for a new record is entered. This makes a good primary key field as each number is unique for each record. However, as a consequence, you cannot edit this number and, if you later delete a record, that number is 'lost'. In other words, once a number has been used it cannot be reused for another record. This data type is used primarily to give uniqueness to each record – for example, a membership number or a product identification number.
- *Date/Time:* Fairly obviously this accommodates dates and times. Although dates and times are composed of numbers, they have special formats. This can be useful

9

for displaying, say, dates, and for when calculations or comparisons need to be performed on these dates. For example you might need to select all clients who joined after a specified date. A variety of standard display formats are available, or you can customise and create your own date format. An example of a date field is: 'date of joining'.

■ *Currency:* Currency data type is used for money. Again, although money may be expressed as numbers, these numbers need to be handled in a special way. The Number data type should not be used for currency values because numbers to the right of the decimal may be rounded during calculations. The Currency data type maintains a fixed number of digits to the right of the decimal. Currency data types are widely used in financial applications. The example in our application is 'annual fee'.

■ *Yes/No:* This data type is used when a field can take one only of two values, such as 'Yes/No', 'True/False', 'On/Off'. This is used for the smoker/non-smoker field.

■ *Memo:* Memo data type is used for lengthy text and numbers, such as might be encountered in electronic documents or case notes. A Memo field can contain up to 32,000 characters. Another example of the use of memo fields is: comments about a hotel in a travel company's database.

■ *OLE:* OLE stands for 'Object Linking and Embedding', and this allows non-textual data (such as pictures or sound clips) to be stored as a field in a database record. OLE is important in databases in which the basic access is via the textual part of the record but where the database also includes valuable multi-media elements.

Choosing data types

Think about the following questions:

1 What would be the effect of rounding on currency (money) data?

2 What data type do you think you would choose for the following fields?

■ **Status**
■ **Last Name**
■ **Street**
■ **Telephone No**
■ **Date of Birth**
■ **Fitness Interests**

3 Later you will find we use a 'Yes/No' field for **Gender**. Explain this!

4 Why would you use a text field for a **Post code**?

Designing a table

Consider creating a table listing hotels in a town for a tourist information centre. What fields would you choose for each record, and what field names would you choose for them? Which data types would you choose for them? What field or combination of fields would make each record in such a table different from every other record? (It might be helpful to collect a brochure from a travel agent that shows a number of hotels in order to see the information they use to inform travellers about the characteristics of hotels.)

Creating a new database

Topic objectives

An Access database file is used to store all the components of an Access database, (tables, queries, forms and reports) which you will meet as you follow this book. The first element of a database you must create is a table. You can create more than one table in a database, and these are essential for the holding of the data and for the generation of queries, forms and reports.

The creation of a table requires the definition of the fields in the table. Each field requires a name to distinguish it from the other fields, and also the type of data that is to be stored in the field needs to be defined.

This topic will show you how to:

- create a new database
- create a table and its component parts
- define data types for fields
- save and open a database.

11

Creating the Total Health and Fitness database and its Client table

A new database is used to store the table (and all queries, forms and reports) that are needed to provide information from the table. To begin with, our database will hold the table of data needed for the leisure centre example.

1 Either start Access by clicking on the **START** button in the Task bar, selecting **PROGRAMS** and selecting **MICROSOFT ACCESS** or, if you have a shortcut icon on your desktop for Access, then you may double-click on it to start Access.

Microsoft Access 2000

2 Choose the **CREATE A NEW DATABASE USING BLANK DATABASE OPTION**. If Access is already running, choose **FILE – NEW** and double-click on the **BLANK DATABASE** icon.

Database

3 In the **NEW DATABASE** dialog box, select the drive and folder in which you wish to store your database. If you do not change folder your database is likely to be stored in the 'My Documents' folder.

4 In the **FILE NAME** box give the database the filename **Total Health and Fitness**. Access will give it the extension of **.mdb**.

5 Click on the **CREATE** button. You have just created a new database and the database window, as illustrated in Figure 3.1, should be open.

6 If the **TABLES** object type is not selected as shown in Figure 3.1, then click on it. The next stage in the construction of the database is to create the table that holds the client details. This table is the main repository of data in the Total

Health and Fitness database. Before any data can be entered this **Client** table needs to be defined. This means specifying the fields that will make up the records in the **Client** table and defining the type of data that will be stored in those fields.

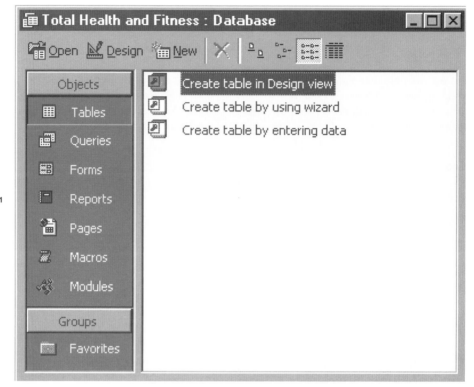

FIGURE 3.1

12

⑦ Double click on **CREATE A NEW TABLE IN DESIGN VIEW**. Alternatively click on the **NEW** button in the table window to display the **NEW TABLE** dialog box. Select **DESIGN VIEW** and click on **OK** (Figure 3.2).

FIGURE 3.2

8 The **TABLE** design window should be displayed (Figure 3.3). Through the **TABLE** design window you define the structure of your table. This is done by filling in the 'Field Name', 'Data Type' and 'Description' cells and by setting 'Field Properties'.

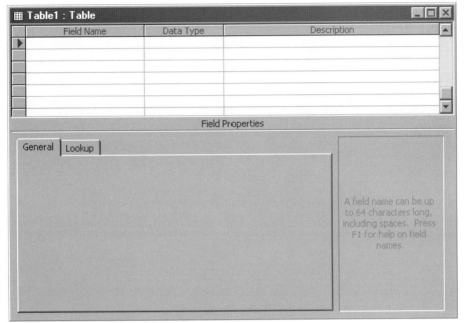

FIGURE 3.3

13

9 The next step is to define the fields for the **Client** table. The name, data type and description (optional) for each field is entered into the Table Design window. At this stage it is important to realise we are *not* entering data but the *definition* of the fields.

10 Enter **Client No** for the first field name. Avoid typing a full stop after 'No' as these are not allowed in field names (see 'Field names and sizes').

11 Move to the **DATA TYPE** column by pressing **ENTER** and click on the down arrow button, which displays the Data Type list box (Figure 3.4). Note: to move between cells you have a choice of pressing either **ENTER**, **TAB**, → or by clicking in the required cell in the grid.

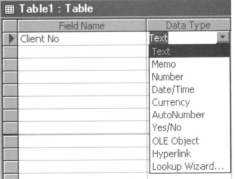

FIGURE 3.4

12 Choose the data type 'AutoNumber'. An AutoNumber type is one in which Access will automatically enter sequential numbers, record by record. This ensures each record will have a unique number in this field. Press **ENTER** to move to the **DESCRIPTION** column. Key in the description as shown in the table. Press **ENTER** to move to the next row (see 'Field descriptions').

Field Name	Data Type	Description
Client No	AutoNumber	Automatic client numbering
Status	Number	Categories are: 1 – Adult Gold; 2 – Adult Silver; 3 – Adult Family; 4 – Child Family; 5 – Business; 6 – Social
Last Name	Text	
First Name	Text	
Title	Text	
Street	Text	
Town	Text	
County	Text	
Post Code	Text	
Telephone No	Text	
Profession	Text	
Date of Birth	Date/Time	
Date of Joining	Date/Time	
Date of Last Renewal	Date/Time	
Fitness Interests	Memo	
Smoker	Yes/No	
Gender	Yes/No	
Photo	OLE Object	

13 Continue to enter the field definitions shown above. Where there is no description, press **ENTER** to take you to the field name column of the next row. The table will be revisited later to set

FIGURE 3.5

individual field properties.

Row Selector

⊞ **Client : Table**

	Field Name
	Client No
	Status

14 Before saving the table a primary key will be defined (see 'What is a primary key?'). Click on the row selector for **Client No** and click on the **PRIMARY KEY** button in the toolbar (Figure 3.5).

15 Once the structure of the table has been designed it needs to be saved. Access uses this information to set up templates through which you will later enter data into the table. To save the table use **FILE–SAVE**. In the **SAVE AS** dialog box, in the Table Name box type the name **Client**. Note that the name that you choose may be 255 characters long and contain any alphanumeric text.

16 Close the table using **FILE – CLOSE**. (Shortcut key **CTRL-W**).

Database tables

The table you have just created is saved as part of the database file and its name will distinguish it from other tables that you will subsequently create that will also be stored in this database file. Access allows you the same freedom for naming tables as Windows does for naming files. You will also find this true for naming other database objects such queries, forms, and reports as all these are stored in one database file.

14

Make use of this freedom to give meaningful names to tables as they will be used later in queries, forms and reports and it is important to be able to recognise the name of the table you require.

Database filenames

The Windows operating system allows you to give long descriptive filenames to files when you are saving them. The complete path to the file (including drive letter, folder path name and filename) can contain up to 255 characters. Any characters may be used except the following: * ? ; \ / : " | < >. You should avoid the use of a period (full stop) as it is used to separate the filename from the extension. You probably will not see the extension when you are working with your files as the Windows operating system generally hides them. Note that Access stores all tables, forms, queries, reports, etc. in this one file.

Closing and opening a database

You can close the database when you have finished working with it using **FILE – CLOSE**. Access will prompt you to save the database if you have made changes that you have not saved.

An existing database is opened from Access using **FILE – OPEN** or by clicking on the **OPEN** button on the toolbar. Select the drive and folder in which your database is stored and select the filename and click on the **OPEN** button.

When you wish to close Access use **FILE – EXIT**. Next time you start Access you will see your database, **Total Health and Fitness** listed in the **OPEN AN EXISTING DATABASE** section of the **MICROSOFT ACCESS** dialog box. Simply highlight the name and click on **OK** to open the database.

15

Closing and opening tables

To close a table, either double-click on the table's control menu button, or choose **FILE–CLOSE**.

You can open an existing table in either Design view or Datasheet view. So far we have considered only the Design view of a table. To open a table in Design view, check the **TABLES** object type is selected in the Database window. Select the table you want to open (for example, the table **Client**), and then click on the **DESIGN** button in the Database window toolbar.

Field names and sizes

Fields need names, lengths and data types to be defined. Access allows field names to be up to 64 characters long with spaces. Field names should be meaningful so the data is easier to work with. Some characters are not allowed in field names. These are, full stops (.), exclamation marks (!) and square brackets ([]).

Why can't you give the same name to more than one field?

The length of a field may be predetermined according to the data type chosen for that particular field. If a data type of date has been chosen, it will have a standard length. You can specify the field size of other data types, such as text and number. If a text field is being used to hold the titles of videos, for example, you need to estimate the length of the longest video title and set the size of the field accordingly.

Field descriptions

A description for a field may be added optionally into the description column in the table's Design view. A description can be up to 255 characters in length. It can be used to provide additional information about a particular field.

Correcting mistakes in field name, description or data type

Point and click in the cell containing the mistake. Correct the mistake in a normal fashion by inserting or deleting text at the insertion point. Click back in the current cell to continue working. Click on the data type cell concerned. Open the list box and select the correct data type.

16

What is a primary key?

The primary key is a field or combination of fields that uniquely identifies each record in a table. It is essential to set up a primary key, if, later, you wish to link this table to other tables that you may add to your database. In the **Client** table the **Client No** is the primary key. Each record has a different number as every client's number will be different. The AutoNumber setting will take care of entering a unique number into this field when the data is entered later on.

If you create a table and do not specify a primary key, when you save the table Access will ask you whether you want to create a primary key (Figure 3.6).

FIGURE 3.6

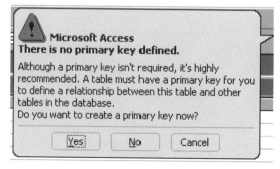

If you choose **NO** the table will be saved without a primary key and if you do not intend to link it to other tables and it serves your purpose, there is no need for a primary key. If you think the table

Table1 : Table	
Field Name	Data Type
ID	AutoNumber
Field 1	Text
Field 2	Text

FIGURE 3.7

should have a primary key field added, choose **YES**. Access will create a field called **ID** with an AutoNumber setting that assigns a unique number to each record (Figure 3.7).

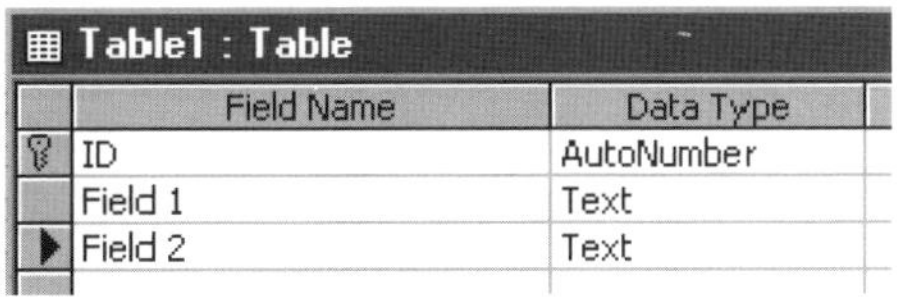

Setting or changing the primary key

To set or change the primary key, with a table open in Design view, select the field or fields you want to define as the primary key. To select one field, click the row selector. To select multiple fields, hold down the Ctrl key, and click the row selectors for each field. Click on the **PRIMARY KEY** button on the tool bar, or choose **EDIT – PRIMARY KEY**. Microsoft Access places the primary key icon in the row selector column.

17

Field properties

Topic objectives

As well as name, data type and size, other properties can be assigned to fields. You can revisit the properties of the fields in your tables at any stage in your database construction once the initial structure of a table has been set up.

This topic will show you how to:

- define field properties
- use a lookup table for a field
- print the table definition and field properties
- create additional tables for this application.

Defining field properties

The basic data type for each field was determined in the previous topic and, by setting the field properties, you can specify how you want data stored, handled and displayed for each field in more detail. For example, if the data type is text you can specify the length of the field (i.e. number of characters allowed – see 'Field properties').

1 Open the **Total Health and Fitness** database. In the **DATABASE WINDOW** select **Client** and click on the **DESIGN** button to open the **Client** table in design view.

2 Select the field **Status**, which has a data type of Number. You will see the Field Properties section in the lower left-hand area of the design window (Figure 4.1). In this field the data that will be entered is a number between 1 and 6 inclusive, as there are 6 status categories. As the Byte number type (see 'Field size property') allows for the storage of whole numbers up to 255, it is a good choice for the number property of the 'Status' field.

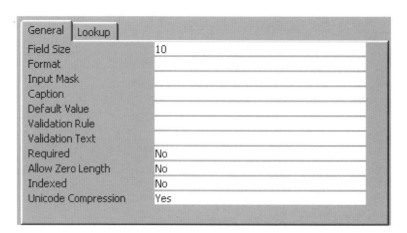

FIGURE 4.1

General	Lookup
Field Size	10
Format	
Input Mask	
Caption	
Default Value	
Validation Rule	
Validation Text	
Required	No
Allow Zero Length	No
Indexed	No
Unicode Compression	Yes

18

3 Click in the **FIELD SIZE** box, open its associated list and select 'Byte'.

4 Select the field **Last Name**.

5 Click in the **FIELD SIZE** box, delete the default size of 50 and replace it with 25.

6 Alter the sizes of the other text fields as follows:

First Name   30
Title   10
Street   30
Town   25
County   20
Post Code   10
Telephone No   12

7 You can assign default values to fields in your table that Access will automatically enter into that field when a new record is created. Specifying your own default values for fields can save time when entering data (see 'Defaults'). Select the **Town** field and in the **DEFAULT VALUE** box key in *Harrogate*

8 Select the **County** field and put *Yorkshire* into its **DEFAULT VALUE** box. Why do think these defaults are set? For more on defaults, see later in this topic.

9 For a database to be useful, data entered into it must be accurate. However, even the most experienced data entry operators can make mistakes. To try to detect mistakes you can test the data entered by creating validation rules. These are simple tests, which are entered as short expressions into the **VALIDATION RULE** text box (see 'Validation'). Select **Status** and click in the **VALIDATION RULE** box and key in *<=6* to prevent an incorrect entry in this field.

10 If the data entered breaks the validation rule, a message box will be displayed to inform the operator the data is incorrect. The message in the message box is defined by the text you put in the **VALIDATION TEXT** text box. Key in the message *Please enter a status number between 1 and 6* into the **VALIDATION TEXT** box for the **Status** field.

11 To prevent a number less than 1 being entered, modify the validation rule to read *<=6 And >0*

12 By setting the **REQUIRED** property of a field to **YES** you will need to make an entry in that particular field for every record. Where it is not necessary to have an entry, this property can be left as its default value. For the fields **Status, Last Name** and **Date of Joining**, in turn, open the **REQUIRED** list box and select **YES**. Consider the reasons for insisting this data must be present.

13 Select the **Date of Birth** field and, in the Format box key in the format *d/m/yyyy* (to suppress leading zeros on day and month) or *dd/mm/yyyy* (to display leading zeros). Repeat this for the two other date fields. Note that the Short date option in the drop-down list of the Format box is of the form 'd/m/yy'. (See 'Creating custom display formats'.)

14 Save the changes using **FILE – SAVE** and close the table using **FILE – CLOSE**.

19

Lookup Wizard

Where a field has a standard choice of entries these can be entered using the Lookup Wizard, as indicated below:

1 Open the **Client** table in Table design view and select the field **Title**.

2 Open the Data type list box and choose 'Lookup Wizard'. Choose the **I WILL TYPE THE VALUES THAT I WANT** option and click on **NEXT>**. Accept the number of columns as 1 and, into the column, key in suitable titles as illustrated in Figure 4.2.

FIGURE 4.2

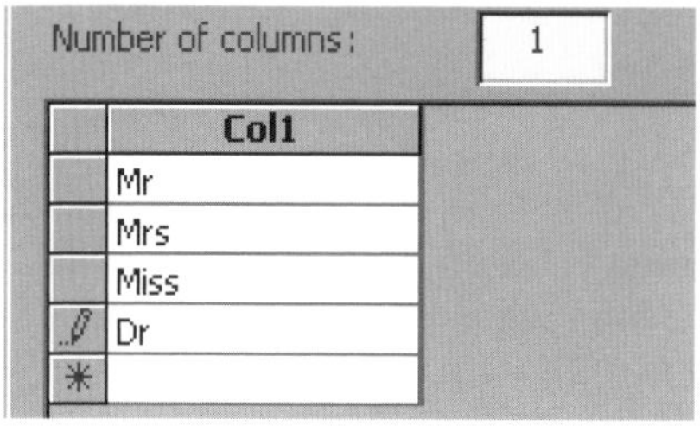

| Number of columns: | 1 |

Col1
Mr
Mrs
Miss
Dr

3 Click on **NEXT>** and **FINISH**. Later, when you come to enter data into this field, you will see it has a drop-down list facility allowing you to choose from the list.

20

Making a printed copy of the table design

Access allows you to view and print the design characteristics (definition) of your tables, forms, queries and reports. To make a printed copy of the table design:

1 Choose **TOOLS – ANALYZE**, and then click **DOCUMENTOR**. Note: You may need to install Access's analysing tools by following the on-screen instructions and putting your Office 2000 disk in your CD reader.

2 Click on the tab corresponding to the type of database object you want to document and view or print. In this case choose the **TABLE** tab.

3 Click in the check box of each table for which definitions are required. Tick the **Client** table.

4 Click **OPTIONS** to specify which features of the selected object or objects you want to print, and then click on **OK**. For the **Client** table try: 'Include for Table: Properties and Relationships'; 'Include for Fields: Names, Data types, Sizes and Properties'; 'Include for Indexes: Names and Fields'.

5 Click on **OK** to exit the **PRINT TABLE DEFINITION** window, then click on **OK** again. Be prepared that Access may take a little time to compile the definition.

6 You might want to check the length of your definition in the **PRINT PREVIEW** window because some definitions can be many pages long.

7 To print the definition, click on the **PRINT** button in the toolbar.

Creating additional tables

So far only one table has been created in the **Total Health and Fitness** database. Historically, database software for PCs was only able to manage one table, and such databases were called 'flat-file' systems. A relational database such as Access can manage more than one table and, by linking the tables, the data can be managed much more efficiently and effectively. At this stage we will just create the other tables we will be using. Linking them will be dealt with in Topic 22.

The other tables required are **Reservation**, **Client Status** and **Session**. The **Reservation** table records details of bookings made of the centre's facilities, the **Client Status** table records the different types of status a client can have and the associated fee for that status, and the **Session** table records details of fitness classes run by the centre. Create these tables using the definitions below:

1 To create a **Reservation** table, click on the **NEW** button in the **DATABASE** window to open the table design window (you may wish to refer back to Topic 3). Define the field types as shown.

2 Define **Reservation No** as the primary key. Save the table as **Reservation**:

Field Name	Data Type
Reservation No	AutoNumber
Location	Text
Client/Session	Yes/No
Client No	Number
Session No	Number
Date	Date/Time
Time	Date/Time

3 Amend the field properties as shown. Save and close the table.

Field	Property	Setting
Location	Field Size	20
	Required	Yes
Client/Session	Required	Yes
Client No	Field Size	Long Integer
	Default value	=Null
Session No	Field Size	Long Integer
	Default value	=Null
Date	Format	d/m/yy
	Required	Yes
Time	Format	Short time
	Required	Yes

4 Now create the **Client Status** table:

Field Name	Data Type	Description
Status	Number	A one-digit identification number
Status Type	Text	Categories are Adult Gold, Adult Silver, Adult Family, Child Family, Business, Social
Fee	Currency	

21

5 Define **Status** as the primary key. Set the field properties as shown below. Save the table as **Client Status** and close.

Field	Property	Setting
Status	Field Size	Byte
	Required	Yes
Status Type	Field Size	15
	Required	Yes
Fee	Required	Yes

6 Now create the **Session** table:

Field Name	Data Type
Session No	AutoNumber
Session Day	Number
Session Time	Date/Time
Instructor	Text
Activity	Text
Gender Mix	Text

7 Define **Session No** as the primary key. Set the properties below and save the table as **Session** and close. Note that **Session Day** has been chosen to be numeric with 1 representing Sunday to 7 representing Saturday. This makes it easier to list sessions in day and time order.

Field	Property	Setting
Session Day	Field Size	Byte
	Required	Yes
Session Time	Format	Short time (equivalent to hh:mm)
	Required	Yes
Instructor	Field Size	30
Activity	Field Size	20
	Required	Yes
Gender Mix	Field Size	10
	Validation Rule	"Male" or "Female" or "Mixed"
	Validation Text	Please enter Male, Female or Mixed

Field properties

Properties for individual fields are set using the field properties section. The data type chosen for the field will determine available options. The table below lists the field properties for a text data type (note: these will vary for other data types):

Property	Description
Field Size	Text field: maximum length. Number field: Number type
Format	Data display: use built-in formats or customise your own
Input Mask	Data entry pattern
Caption	Text that will appear in the field label in a form or report

Default Value	A value for the field that is automatically entered when records are created
Validation Rule	A rule or expression that is used to test data being entered
Validation Text	If invalid data has been entered this text will be displayed
Required	Specifies whether or not a data entry must be made into the field
Allow Zero Length	Allows you to store a zero length string (" ") to indicate data that exists but is unknown.
Indexed	Single-field indexes to speed up searches

Field size property

The maximum size of data that can be entered into a field is defined by this property. For a text field, enter a number less than 255, which specifies the number of alphanumeric characters needed. Choose the field size by considering the length of the longest text data that is to be entered into the field. The default size setting for a text field is 50.

If a number data type property is chosen, the following choice of field size properties is available:

Setting	Description
Byte	Suitable for the storage of whole numbers with values between 0 and 255. Occupies 1 byte
Integer	Suitable for storage of whole numbers with values between $-32,768$ and 32,767. Occupies 2 bytes
Long Integer	Suitable for storage of numbers from $-2,147,483,648$ to 2,147,483,647 (no fractions). Occupies 4 bytes
Single	Suitable for storage of numbers with six digits of precision, from $-3.402823E38$ to 3.402823E38. Occupies 4 bytes
Double (Default)	Suitable for storage of numbers with ten digits of precision, from $-1.79769313486232E308$ to 1.79769313486232E308. Occupies 8 bytes
Decimal	Suitable for storage of numbers from -10^{38} to 10^{38}. Occupies 12 bytes (decimal precision 28 places)

Default values of numeric fields

If you do not specify a default value, the default value for number, currency and yes/no fields is zero; in the case of yes/no fields, zero means 'no'. Text, memo and date fields are empty by default.

You can specify a default field using text or an expression. When users add records to the table, they can either accept this value or enter a different value when the default is not appropriate. If, for example, a sales table contains the field 'Date paid', the expression '=Date()' can be used to put the current date into this field.

Validation

The maximum length for both the **VALIDATION RULE** and the **VALIDATION TEXT** boxes is 255 characters. When data is entered or amended, the validation is performed. Validations are often concerned with numeric fields (e.g. a credit limit that cannot be greater than a certain value). Fields with other data types may also be validated (for example, a date may only be entered in a certain time period or a stock code can be checked to see if it is a valid stock code).

Formatting data display

Data can be displayed using custom formats which will display it in the format specified. For example, a display format can be created that will display text in upper case regardless of data being entered in lower or upper case. A custom format is created using a template, as illustrated below:

Numeric format

Examples are:

##,###.00 (66.12   7.30   5,890.07   300.00)

#0.000   (34.407   0.040)

\# displays a digit if only if one is entered

0 displays either the digit entered or 0

, used as a thousands separator

Date format

Examples are:

dddd d mmmm yyyy   Sunday 23 April 2000

dd/mm/yy   23/04/00

d-m-yy   2-5-00 (this format does not display leading zeros).

d displays the day of the month number without leading zeros; dd displays the day of the month number with leading zeros; ddd displays the abbreviated weekday text; dddd displays the full weekday text. Similarly m for month. yy displays the last two digits of year; yyyy displays the full year number.

Time format

Example:

h:mm   AM/PM   (8:16 PM)

hh:mm:ss   (10:11:23)

h displays hours without leading zeros; hh displays hours with leading zeros. Similarly m for minutes and s for seconds. The colon separates hours, minutes and seconds. AM/PM or am/pm displays time in 12 instead of 24 hour format.

Text format

Example:

(@@@@@) @@@@@@   (01777) 565656

@ indicates a character is required in the particular position. The 'greater than' symbol > displays text in uppercase and the 'less than' symbol < displays text in lowercase.

Creating input masks

Data entry can be made simpler by creating an input mask, which is a particular format or pattern in which the data is entered. An input mask is only suitable where all the data for that particular field has the same pattern (for example, stock numbers like NEC-321-6090-J). To illustrate the creation of an input mask, some examples are shown in the following table:

Input Mask	Sample Values
\NEC-000-0000->L	NEC-321-6090-J
00009-0000999	01345-678902, 0777-567899
>L<????????????????	Wakefield
>L?99 9a??	AB1 2CD

A mask is created using special mask symbols:

Mask character	Indicates
0	a number (digit) must be entered
9	a digit may be entered
#	a digit, + or − sign or space may be entered
L	a letter must be entered
?	a letter may be entered
A	a letter or digit must be entered
A	a letter or digit may be entered
&	any character or space must be entered
C	any character or space may be entered
. , : - /	decimal point, thousands, date and time separators
<	characters to right are converted to lower case
>	characters to right are converted to upper case
\	The character following is **not** to be interpreted as a mask character
!	Causes the input mask to display from right to left rather than from left to right. Characters keyed in to the mask always fill it from left to right. You can include the exclamation point anywhere in the input mask

Revisit the properties of the **Last Name** field and set the mask using the fifth example illustrated above. Check you use the correct number of question marks (i.e. 24, one less than the field width of 25). For the **Post Code** field try out the fourth example of an input mask. You may also wish to set either a format or mask for the telephone number.

TOPIC 5

Data entry and editing

Topic objectives

Having created the table structures, the next stage is to enter data into the tables. Data can also be entered through queries and, more importantly, forms. Here you will see that entering data via a table is very straightforward.

This topic will show you how to:

■ open a table in Datasheet view and enter data into the datasheet
■ move around the datasheet so data can be edited.

Data entry

In the preceding topics we have worked with tables in Design view only. For data entry, a table needs to be opened in Datasheet view.

Whether you open a table in Design or Datasheet view, it is easy to switch from the Datasheet view to the Design view and vice versa. If you make changes to the table structure in Design view, you will be asked to save them if you switch back to the datasheet view. Use the button on the toolbar for switching between the views:

When in Design view		When in Datasheet view	
Datasheet view button		Design view button	

In Datasheet view, the headings of the columns are the field names you previously defined. Each row in the datasheet is a record and, as you complete each record, it is automatically saved into the table.

Entering client data

To open a table in Datasheet view:

1 Open the **Total Health and Fitness** database. In the Database window, if the **TABLE** object type is not selected, click on it.

2 Double-click on the **Client** table or select the **Client** table, and choose the **OPEN** button. The table will open in Datasheet view. Notice there are some fields already filled with the values you set as defaults. You can enter an alternative value or do nothing, thereby accepting the default value. Note, you could delete the value to leave the field blank if the required property is not set.

3 Do not enter a value into the **Client No** field but press **ENTER** to move to the next field. This is an AutoNumber field and, if you do try to enter data into it, the entry will not be accepted. Let Access number all the Client number fields.

4 Enter the data for the **Client** table as shown in the Appendix. After entering the data for each field, move to the next by pressing **ENTER**, **TAB** or **→**. When entering the data for the logical fields use a tick to indicate Smoker or Male (blank is Non-smoker or Female). When you press **ENTER** after entering data into the last field of a record, Access saves the record.

5 While you are entering the data, try testing the validation rules (those Access applies and those that have been defined). Try entering text into a date type field. Access expects the correct data type, and the Office Assistant will inform you of your mistake (see Figure 5.1).

FIGURE 5.1

6 Try entering a **Status** number greater than 6. This will test the validation rule set up in the field properties for **Status** (Figure 5.2).

27

FIGURE 5.2

7 Skip fields that are blank (see below for more details about data validation, editing data and using **UNDO**).

Data validation
Data is validated on entry. If it does not conform to the data type set for that field an error message will be generated. If the data entered breaks any validation rule that has been set as a property for that field, if there is validation text, this appears as the error message.

Fields without data (null values)
Sometimes not all the data for a record is available (for example, the telephone number may be missing). To skip a field, simply press **ENTER** or **TAB** to take you to the next field. It is acceptable to skip fields where the data is not vital but, for data such as the **Last Name**, it is not acceptable.

Where a field is left without an entry it is said to be *null* (i.e. there is nothing there). If you perform mathematical calculations on numeric fields, Access ignores fields containing nulls.

Undo

If you use the wrong command by mistake or something unexpected happens, always try **EDIT** – **UNDO** or click on the **UNDO** button before doing anything else.

Editing data

When the records have been entered into a table, this data is available to be used, as is evident in the following topics. The data in the datasheet can be checked and, if necessary, any errors corrected.

Moving around records

You can move around records in the datasheet by using either **EDIT** – **GO TO**, the | **UP** and **DOWN ARROW** keys, **PAGE UP** and **PAGE DOWN** keys or the vertical scroll bar. However, the most efficient way to move around records in large databases is with the navigation buttons in the lower-left corner of the window.

Navigation buttons and record indicators

In the status bar of the datasheet window are the navigation buttons and record indicators. The record number of the currently selected record is displayed.

To move to	Click
First record	|◀
Last record	▶|
Previous record	◀
Next record	▶
New record	▶*
Specific record	Click in record counter box [1] (or press **F5**), type the record number you want, and then press **ENTER**.

Selecting data in the datasheet

Various parts of the datasheet can be selected, as described below:

To select	Do this
A single field	Move the pointer to the left-hand side of a cell so it changes shape into a white cross and click
A word in a field	Double-click on the word

A record	Click in the record selector at the left edge of the record, or choose **EDIT – SELECT RECORD**
More than one record	Click and drag in the record selector edge for the required number of records
A field column	Click on the column heading (the field name at the top of the column)
Several field columns	Click on the first column heading required for the selection and drag to the last

Moving and copying fields

A field may be moved, by selecting it, using **EDIT – CUT**, clicking in the cell where the field is to be moved to and using **EDIT – PASTE**.

A field may be copied, by selecting it, using **EDIT – COPY**, clicking in the cell where the copy is required and using **EDIT – PASTE**. Alternatively you may prefer to use the cut, copy and paste ✂ 📋 📋 buttons.

Moving and copying records

A complete table or a selected set of records of a table can be copied to other tables or within the existing table via the clipboard. It is possible to hold up to 12 clips on the clipboard. Records may be moved and copied using **EDIT – CUT/COPY** and **EDIT – PASTE**. Generally moving isn't an operation you would need to carry out within the same table as the records can be displayed in any order chosen. Moving and also copying can be carried out between databases providing the table structures are similar.

One instance where copying is useful is for making a backup of a table. Should you decide to revise the data types of fields in a table, it is advisable to make a backup of the table first in case mistakes are made that could result in the loss of data.

29

Backing up a table

Using copy and paste, a backup of the **Client** table will be made:

1. Choose **TABLES** in the **DATABASE WINDOW**.

2. Select the table **Client** and choose **EDIT – COPY**.

3. Next, create a database to hold the backup by choosing **FILE – NEW**, selecting the folder in which the backup file is to be stored, keying *THF backup* in the **FILE NAME** box and clicking on **CREATE**. This database is now active.

4. Choose **EDIT – PASTE** and in the **TABLE NAME** box of the **PASTE TABLE AS** dialog box key in *Client backup*

5. Check the default option **STRUCTURE AND DATA** is selected before clicking on **OK**.

6. Use **FILE – CLOSE** to close the backup database.

If this backup is needed to restore a damaged file, open the backup database, select and copy the table, open the normal database (use **FILE – OPEN**) and paste as described above.

Note: You can also use **FILE – EXPORT** and **FILE – GET EXTERNAL DATA** to perform this backup operation (see Topic 24) or, alternatively, you may back up the entire database by first closing it and switching to Explorer (or My Computer) and copying the file to another folder or to floppy disk or other backup medium.

Adding photographs

In the **Client** table a field **Photograph** of type OLE object has been created. OLE stands for 'Object Linking and Embedding'. In the **Photograph** field a link to a client's image file can be stored and this photograph can be displayed in a form or report. As we are entering data in the **Client** table datasheet, we will leave creating this kind of link until we have created a form for the **Client** table in Topic 11. If after adding links to image files you view the **Client** table in datasheet view, Access will display the name of the object type (for example, bitmap image).

Working with data

Topic objectives

The accuracy of the information a database can produce is dependent on the accuracy of the data stored in the tables. It is difficult to eliminate all errors, such as mistakes of transcription or keying in, even using data validation techniques. The data itself is in a constant state of flux: new clients enrol or existing ones may change their addresses. Simple changes can be made using the Find technique described below and old records can be deleted. Where text fields are used to store descriptions such as profession or fitness interests, it is useful to be able to spellcheck the entries.

This topic will show you how to:

- use the spell checker
- delete records
- use find and replace to edit data
- customise the display of data in the datasheet and to print data
- amend field size and type.

Editing data

Using the **Client** table, we shall experiment with the data management techniques mentioned:

1 Open the **Client** table in Datasheet view. With a table open in Datasheet view you can spell check the whole table or, more usually, a selection of data in the datasheet. Select the **Fitness Interests** column and spell check it by clicking on the **SPELLING** button. The spell checker will prompt you to correct words that it does not recognise.

2 Add a new record by clicking on the **NEW RECORD** ▶* button at the bottom of the window. This record is shown below:

Status	Last Name	First Name	Title	Street	Town	County
2	Adams	Eleanor	Miss	70 Wellfield Row	Harrogate	Yorkshire

Post Code	Date of Birth	Date of Joining	Date of Last Renewal	Fitness interests	Smoker	Gender
YO2 7GE	8/10/72	2/4/00	2/4/00	Swimming, Judo	☐	☐

3 If you wish to find or find and replace a particular entry in a certain field, first make that field current by clicking in that column. Click in the **Telephone No** field of the first record.

4 Choose **EDIT – FIND** or click on the **FIND** 🔍 button in the toolbar. The Find and Replace dialog box is displayed with the Find tab selected.

5 Key **01435** in to the **FIND WHAT** box and select **START OF FIELD** in the **MATCH** box (Figure 6.1).

FIGURE 6.1

6 Click on the **FIND NEXT** button. This should highlight the first occurrence of a telephone number with this code. Click on the **FIND NEXT** button to find other matches.

7 Now click on the **REPLACE** tab of the **FIND AND REPLACE** dialog box. Key **01436** in to the **REPLACE WITH** box. Keep the other settings as for the Find operation. Click on the **REPLACE ALL** button. Answer **YES** to continue but note that, at this point, you could abandon the operation.

8 Now replace all **01436** codes with **01435**.

9 Select the last record, which you have just created, and delete it.

Deleting records

A record can be deleted from a table using a datasheet or a form (you will meet forms in Topic 11). To delete records using a datasheet, first display the datasheet. Select the record or records you wish to delete. Press the **DELETE** key (or choose **EDIT – DELETE** from the menu). Access prompts you to confirm the deletion. Choose **OK** to delete the record or **CANCEL** to restore it.

Finding and replacing

To find a particular field (Figure 6.2) key the string (set of characters) you wish to find into the **FIND WHAT** text box, such as the last name 'Wilson'. In the **MATCH:** box select whether your string should match the whole field, any part of the field or the start of the field. In the **SEARCH:** box choose between **UP**, **DOWN** or **ALL**.

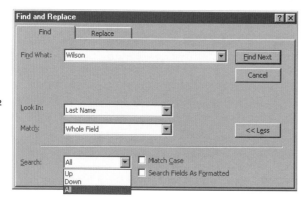

FIGURE 6.2

The **MATCH CASE** check box allows the choice of making your search case-sensitive or not. The **SEARCH FIELDS AS FORMATTED** check box allows the choice of making your search sensitive to formatting (e.g. finding a field as, say, a number 28/3/01 or as it is formatted 28-Mar-01). In the **LOOK IN** box you may choose between limiting your search to the current field or to including all the fields in the table.

Each time a match is found it is highlighted. If either the top or the bottom of the table is reached, Access indicates there are no more matches to be found.

To replace a particular field, click on the **REPLACE** tab or use **EDIT – REPLACE** and the steps are the same as for finding a field, except that in the dialog box there is an additional text box, **REPLACE WITH**, into which the replacement string is entered. Strings can be replaced according to which button is clicked:

Replaces the highlighted string and finds the next occurrence of the **FIND WHAT** string.

Replaces all occurrences of the string without stopping.

Datasheet display: column widths, row heights, fonts and column order

By altering the width of columns and the height of rows in the datasheet the display of data can be tailored to suit your preferences. Usually columns are made smaller, as field widths often err on the large side, and this is easily achieved especially if you are familiar with Windows applications:

1. Open the **Client** table in Datasheet view. To alter the **Street** column width, move the pointer to the field name row at the top of the datasheet, between **Street** and **Town**. The pointer should change shape to a ✛.

2. Click and drag the column to widen it. Try adjusting other column widths of the **Client** datasheet to accommodate the data.

3. To alter the row height, move the pointer to the row selector column at the left of the datasheet, between any two rows. Note, it does not matter which two rows you choose as all rows take on the new height. The pointer should change shape to a ✛.

4. Click and drag to increase the height of all the rows.

5. Choose **FORMAT – FONT** and select a font and size from the **FONT** dialog box. All the data will take on the selected font. Fonts cannot be applied independently to fields. You may wish to use **UNDO** to return to the original font.

6. To rearrange the order in which the columns are shown in the datasheet, a drag and drop method can be used to move them. First, select the field column you wish to move, move the pointer over the selection so that it changes shape to a left-pointing arrow, click (pointer changes shape to drag and drop) and drag the

column to a new position. A darker column dividing line will indicate where the field will go when the mouse button is released. Select the **Fitness Interests** column and drag it to between the **Profession** and the **Date of Birth** columns.

7 Select the **County** column and choose **FORMAT – HIDE COLUMNS**. To redisplay the columns, choose **FORMAT – UNHIDE COLUMNS**. In the dialog box, select the column(s) to be unhidden and click on **CLOSE**.

8 Move the **Last Name** and **Title** columns so they are the first two columns. Select both these columns and choose **FORMAT – FREEZE COLUMNS**. Now scroll to the right across the datasheet and you will see these two columns remaining on screen. Unfreeze these columns by choosing **FORMAT – UNFREEZE ALL COLUMNS**.

9 When you close the table you can choose whether or not to make the layout changes permanent by selecting **Yes** or **No** in the save changes message box. Close the table without choosing.

Data display – sorting

The data in a datasheet will be displayed in 'natural order' – that is, in the order in which the records were entered. This may not be the order in which you would like to see the records. The order in which the records are displayed is controlled using the **SORT ASCENDING** and **SORT DESCENDING** buttons on the toolbar.

To change the displayed order of the records using one field:

1 Open the **Client** table in Datasheet view. Select a column by which you wish to sort (click on the field name at the top of the column). Choose the **Last Name** column.

2 Click on either the **SORT ASCENDING** or **SORT DESCENDING** button. Try this for other fields in the table.

To change the displayed order of the records using more than one field:

3 Select the columns by which you wish to sort (click on the field name at the top of the first column and drag to the last column). Sorting columns must be next to one another with the highest priority being assigned to the leftmost column. If necessary, rearrange the columns in the datasheet.

4 Select the **Status** and **Last Name** columns together and click on the **SORT ASCENDING** button. Note the effect.

5 Drag the **Town** column so it is to the right of the **Status** column, select these two columns and click on the **SORT ASCENDING** button.

6 Drag the **Town** column so it is to the left of the **Status** column. Select these two columns, and click on the **SORT ASCENDING** button. You should see the data is displayed in a different order from the last sort.

7 Close the **Client** table without saving the layout changes.

Printing a table

A table can be printed from its datasheet. Access prints a datasheet as it appears on the screen. It is advisable always to preview your datasheet before printing by choosing **FILE – PRINT PREVIEW** or clicking on the **PRINT PREVIEW** button in the toolbar.

If you need to set up your printer, choose the **SETUP** button in the **PRINT** dialog box:

1 To print the Client datasheet open the **Client** table in Datasheet view.

2 If you intend to print selected records, select those records. To print all the records, select nothing.

3 Choose **FILE – PRINT PREVIEW** and, if the preview is satisfactory, choose **FILE – PRINT** to display the **PRINT** dialog box. Note that all records are previewed.

4 Under **PRINT RANGE**, choose one of the following:

- **ALL** (to print all the records in the table).
- **SELECTED RECORDS** (to print a previously selected set of records).
- **PAGES** (to print specific pages from your table).

If you select **PAGES**, specify the page numbers of the first and last pages you want to print.

5 Set other **PRINT** dialog box options if necessary and click on **OK**. Close the table.

For large datasheets, Access prints from left to right and then from top to bottom. For example, if your datasheet is two pages wide and three pages long, Access prints the top two pages first, then the middle two pages, then the bottom two pages.

Changing field size or type

You may find it necessary to change a field data type as the design of your database develops (for example, a field size may be too small). Before you make any changes to field data types, make a backup copy of the table in case you accidentally lose data because your changes were too great.

Before you make changes consider the following implications:

Numeric fields

Altering the data type to another number type that can hold a larger number is generally safe – for example, changing a data type of byte to that of integer (refer back to Topic 4 for definitions of field size). If, on the other hand, you change to a data type that holds a smaller number (for example, changing from double to integer), your data will be truncated (in this case by losing the decimal part of the number). Truncation means reducing the number of digits in a number to fit the new field size property you choose.

Note: A field cannot be converted into an AutoNumber type field as Access provides automatic numbering in this field type, and this type can be set only when the table is first constructed and has no data entered.

Text fields

If the field size of a text field is altered to make it larger, there is no problem but if the alteration is to make the field size smaller any text that is too long will be truncated. Text fields may be converted to memo fields but if a memo field is converted to a text field it will be truncated to 255 characters.

Conversion between data types

It is possible to convert a field from one data type to another depending on the data held in the field. Converting from number to text, for instance, should present no problem but if you are converting from text to number, check you do not have alphabetic characters in your data. Data will be lost if Access cannot convert it.

Primary key or fields used in relationships

You cannot change the data type or field size property of these fields, unless you first remove the primary key assignation (in the same way as it was applied) and delete any relationships. These can be restored after changes have been made. Relationships are discussed in Topic 22.

To change a field data type, make a backup copy of your table, display the Design view of your table and make the necessary alterations.

Using filters to select records

Topic objectives

Once the data for a set of records has been entered into a table, it can be used to serve the purpose the database was set up for. Commonly, there is a need is to select out particular subsets of data to answer various questions (for example, which records belong to clients in a particular town).

Two methods for selecting data are available in Access: filtering and querying. Querying is the most useful method and queries are an integral part of the database. These are introduced in Topic 8. Filtering is less useful but it is a quick method that allows you to view a selected set of data. To appreciate the similarities and differences of the two methods, it would be useful to revisit this topic after you have completed the topics on queries.

This topic will show you how to:

- use a filter to select records using one field as a criterion (filter by selection)
- use a filter to select records using more than one field as criteria (filter by form).

Filter by selection

A filter created by this method will select records that match the value of the field selected. To filter by this method:

1 Open the table in Datasheet view. Select a field displaying a value that is your criterion by clicking in the field to place the insertion point in it. Click on the **FILTER BY SELECTION** button in the toolbar. Using the **Client** table select Knaresborough in the **Town** column and apply a filter to display only records that satisfy this criterion. The filter control buttons are:

    Filter by selection
    Remove/apply filter

2 The records displayed will be those with the selected value only. Records could be sorted further (say by status), using the sorting buttons on the toolbar.

3 To remove the filter, click on the **REMOVE FILTER** button. Note that, once the filter is removed this button becomes an **APPLY FILTER** button and can be used to reapply the filter.

Filter by form

A filter created by this method will select records that match the value of more than one field. Alternatives may be included (for example, Knaresborough and Spofforth in the **TOWN** field).

1 Click on the **FILTER BY FORM**  button in the toolbar. This displays a filter form. The one illustrated below is for the **Client** table:

⊞ Client: Filter by Form						_ □ ×
Client No	Status	Last Name	First Name	Title	Street	Town
▶						"Knaresborough" ▼
Look for ╱ Or ╱					◀	▶

2 Criteria for record selection are specified using the filter form. When you select a field you can open a drop-down list, which displays all the different values used for that field in the underlying data.

3 You may specify 'and' criteria by setting values in one or more fields (say all women of status 6).

4 One or more 'or' criteria can be set using the **OR** tab. This will display another sheet of the form filter. The rules of 'and' and 'or' logic for data selection are the same as for queries, and are covered in more detail in Topic 9.

5 In the **Town** field select Spofforth. Click on the **OR** tab and select Knaresborough. Click on the **APPLY FILTER** button on the toolbar.

6 To order the records by **STATUS** click in the status column and click on either the **SORT ASCENDING** or **SORT DESCENDING** button.

7 To remove the filter, click on the **REMOVE FILTER** button.

8 The filter can be modified. To do this, click on the **FILTER BY FORM** button to redisplay the form filter.

9 Remove the town criteria by deleting them. Set criteria in the **Status** field to filter out the values 3 or 4 for family clients.

10 Click on the **APPLY FILTER** button to see the records.

11 Experiment with different filter forms, selecting records by setting criteria for different fields.

12 Close the table without saving the changes.

What is a filter?

Filters are used in conjunction with tables, queries and forms as a means of displaying selected records. A filter will 'filter out' only those records that match specified criteria and will display only these records. No records are deleted in the filtering process. Those that are not selected simply do not form part of the displayed data.

When a filter is created it is stored with the table, query or form and can allow the user quickly to view their data using the filter criteria without having to resort to creating a query. Trends in data may be identified using this method of data filtering. Information concerning, for example, poor membership in a certain category or property category, can be easily obtained. Only one filter is stored with the table, query or report but it may be changed if necessary. If you make changes to a filter and do not want to save them when you close the table, query or form, say **NO** to the **SAVE CHANGES?** question.

A datasheet displays all the records in its underlying table and, by attaching a filter, selected records only will be displayed. Using the buttons on the toolbar, the filter can be switched on or off easily.

The advantage a filter offers is it can be designed very quickly whilst viewing the form, table or query. If records are being amended, it can be useful to select certain records (for example, to make a room change for a particular fitness activity).

Modifying a filter

Any filter you create either by selection or by form will be saved with the table – if you save the table. To alter the filter to use a different field value (or values) for selection purposes, simply select that field value and click on the **FILTER BY SELECTION** button or click on the **FILTER BY FORM** button and specify your criteria in the form.

Using a saved filter

If you create a filter and then save the table, the filter is saved with the table. You may close the table and, later, if you open the table, you can apply the filter using **RECORDS – APPLY FILTER/SORT**. Later you will see how to create forms, and filters can be used with forms in exactly the same way as with tables. As the filter is stored with the table or form, you can have a different filter associated with your table from that associated with your form.

39

Selecting data – queries

Topic objectives

The real power of database software is its ability to select relevant data, usually in answer to a question. The data stored in a database is of no use unless it can be retrieved, and only if it can be retrieved in a way so as to be useful. A video rental shop would want to use a database to find out which videos were on loan to avoid wasting a customer's time searching for a tape out on loan.

We have seen how filters can give answers to relatively straightforward questions, such as clients living in certain towns. Queries can do the same but also offer more ways to specify search criteria, and they can be saved for repeated use. Also, forms and reports can be based on queries to display and print selected data. Queries may select data from more than one table (provided the tables are linked) and you will learn about this in Topic 23. Here all the queries will be based on one table, the **Client** table.

This topic will show you how to:

- create queries using the wizard and the Query design window
- save and run a query
- print the data selected by a query
- delete queries.

Query design

Creating a query involves two aspects:

1. Selecting the fields that are to be displayed when the query is run. It is not usually necessary to select all fields (for example, only the name and the date of last renewal of a client may be all that is needed to check subscriptions are up to date).

2. Selecting the records that are to be displayed when the query is run. For this Access provides a method in common with other database management software called 'Query By Example' (QBE). This method lets you specify the values of the data you are looking for, just as in the filter by form method.

Simple Query Wizard

There are different types of query, the 'select' query being the commonest. A select query will select fields from a table. The simple Query Wizard helps you design a simple select query. The wizard will ask you to select the table you wish to query and which fields you want in your query. It will create the query, which you can then modify later using the query design window:

1 In the Database window double-click on **CREATE QUERY BY USING WIZARD**. Alternatively, click on **NEW** and choose **SIMPLE QUERY WIZARD**.

2 In the **TABLE/QUERIES** drop-down list box in the **SIMPLE QUERY WIZARD** dialog box you will see the **Client** table selected. The **TABLE/QUERIES** drop-down list box is used to select the table the query is to be based on.

3 Add the fields **Client No, Last Name, Gender**, and **Date of Joining** to the query by highlighting each field in turn and clicking on the ⟩ button (see 'Adding or removing fields') (Figure 8.1).

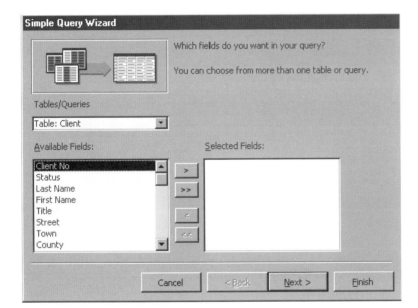

FIGURE 8.1

41

4 Click on **NEXT>**. Select a detail query and click on **NEXT>**. Give the query the title **Dates of Joining** and click on **FINISH**. The result of your query will be shown in Datasheet view.

5 View and close the query window. The name of the query is listed in the Database window.

Adding or removing fields

If you wish to add all the fields to the query, click on the ⟩⟩ button. If you want to add a selected set of fields, highlight each field and click on the ⟩ button. You may change your mind and use the ⟨⟨ button to remove all fields (so you may start again) or use the ⟨ button to remove a selected field.

Query design window

To create a query that will select the required fields and records you ask for, you need to use the query design window (Figure 8.2). This window is in two halves. The upper half is where the table windows of the tables used in the query are displayed. In the lower half is a grid for specifying fields and their associated criteria.

For a simple select query the **FIELD** and **CRITERIA** rows are important. The first row in each column shows the field names of fields chosen for the query (this may be some or all of the fields). In the criteria row an example value of the data may be given. As you work your way through this topic you will be introduced to the function of the other rows in the grid.

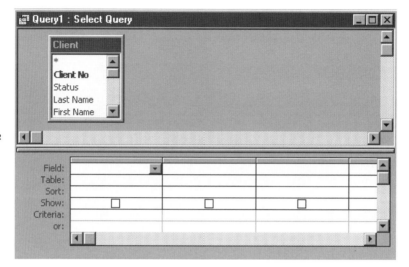

FIGURE 8.2

1 Click on the **QUERIES** object type in the **DATABASE WINDOW** and click on the **NEW** button to create a new query. If you have not created any queries yet, the **OPEN** and **DESIGN** buttons will also allow you to create a new query.

2 Select Design view in the **NEW QUERY** dialog box and click on **OK**.

3 The **SHOW TABLE** dialog box appears in front of the query design window. This dialog box allows you to select all the tables needed for the query.

4 Select the **Client** table and choose **ADD** to add it to the query. Click on the **CLOSE** button.

5 To add all the fields to the query, double-click on the title bar of the **Client** table in the upper section of the window. This selects all the fields.

6 Click on any of the selected fields (not the *) and drag to the field cell in the lower section of the query window. The pointer should look like a set of record cards .

7 When you release the mouse button, all the field names will have been added to the query. Use the horizontal scroll bar to move to the right as all the columns will not fit on the screen.

8 Click on the **RUN** button on the toolbar. You should see the whole of the table displayed. This data is displayed dynamically. It is only a view of the underlying data in the table. Access calls this dynamic view a 'dynaset'.

9 Click on the **DESIGN** button in the toolbar to return to the Query design window.

10 Remove all the fields from the query by selecting all the field columns and pressing **DELETE** (see 'Removing fields from the query').

11 Add fields individually to the query, experimenting with the different methods described below. Add the fields **Client No, Status, Street, Town** and **County**.

12 Click on the **RUN** button and you should see these fields only from all the records of the table forming the dynaset. Click on the **DESIGN** button in the toolbar to return to the query design window.

13 By adding and removing fields you alter the fields in your query so they are **Last Name, Gender, Status** and **Fitness Interests.**

14 Click on the **RUN** ! button to see these fields only from all the records forming the dynaset.

15 Save the query using **FILE – SAVE**, give it the name **Clients' Fitness Interests** and click on **OK**. Close the query and you should see the name of the query in the database window.

Adding all the fields in the table to the query

Double-click on the title bar of the table field list box in the upper section of the window to select all the fields. Click on any of the selected fields (not the *) and drag to the field row in the lower section of the query window and release.

Adding individual fields in the table to the query

There are three alternative ways of adding the fields one by one to a query:

▨ Double-click on the name of the field required in the field list box in the upper section of the window. It will appear in the next available column in the grid below.

▨ Click in the field cell in the lower section of the window. A list box button appears at the end of the cell. Click on the list box button and a drop-down list of field names will appear. Select the name of the field required (if necessary scroll through the list), click on it and it will appear in the field cell.

```
Field:
Table:  Client.*
Sort:   Client No
Show:   Status
Criteria: Last Name
or:     First Name
        Title
        Street
        Town
```

▨ Click on the name of the field required in the field list box in the upper section of the window. Drag and drop this field into the required field cell in the lower part of the query window. While doing this, the pointer should look like one record card. If you drop the field on to a column containing a field, a column will be inserted to contain the new field.

Removing fields from the query

Fields may be removed singly or in blocks from the query. To remove the all the fields from the query, select the first column by clicking on the bar at the top of the column (the pointer will change shape to a down arrow) and drag to select all the columns. Press the **DELETE** key or choose **EDIT – DELETE**.

Tip: After selecting the first column you may prefer the **SHIFT + →** method of selecting additional columns in a more controlled fashion.

To remove an individual field from the query, just select the required column for deleting and use **EDIT – DELETE**.

Displaying the result of a query

Click on the **RUN QUERY** button or the **DATASHEET** button on the toolbar to display the result of a query on screen. To return to the query design, click on the **DESIGN** button next to the **DATASHEET** button in the toolbar:

Design button ▨ ▾   Datasheet button ▦ ▾   Run Query button ❗

Access displays a datasheet containing the records that match the query criteria. This query result is formed only when the query is run and is discarded when the query is closed. A query must work in this way as it needs to work with the current data in its underlying table. Access calls a query result 'a dynaset'. A dynaset is a temporary table and is not a permanent part of your database. If you modify your query or the data in the underlying table, the resulting dynaset will change accordingly.

Saving a query

Often the same question needs to be asked of the database on a regular basis (for example, is a client's subscription due?). A query designed to do this would be saved so it can be used repeatedly.

To save a query, choose **FILE – SAVE** and in the **QUERY NAME** box of the **SAVE AS** dialog box, enter a name that will remind you of what the query is about. The name can be up to 255 characters. Click on **OK**. You will see the name of your query in the queries list of the **DATABASE** window, from where it can be opened for use on another occasion.

Closing and opening a query

To close a query, either double-click on the query's control menu button or choose **FILE – CLOSE**.

An existing query can be opened in either Design view or Datasheet view. In the database window, select the **QUERIES** object type. Select the query you want to open, and then click on the **DESIGN** button to open it in Design view or the **OPEN** button to open it in Datasheet view.

Query creation practice

Create a series of queries showing all the records in the database but including the following fields only:

- Client No, Last Name, First Name, Telephone No.
- Client No, Date of Joining.
- Profession.

Examine each of the dynasets in turn. Do not save these queries. Consider in what circumstances each of these lists may be useful.

Printing a query

1 Before printing the dynaset produced by your query, it is advisable to preview it first. From the database window, open the query **Clients' Fitness Interests** in datasheet view.

2 Click on the **PRINT PREVIEW** 🔍 button on the toolbar. You will be shown a preview that displays a miniature version of what is to be printed.

3 The pointer becomes a magnifying glass and can be use to zoom in to the page. Clicking will toggle between zoom-in and zoom-out modes.

4 Some columns may need widening. Click on **CLOSE** to return to the datasheet and widen the columns (refer back to Topic 6).

5 Preview again, zoom in to check the columns are wide enough, click on the **PRINT** button.

6 Click on **OK** in the **PRINT** dialog box to print the dynaset.

7 Click on the **CLOSE** button to return to the datasheet view and close the query

Note: Clicking the right mouse button will give a shortcut menu of preview and printing commands.

Page Setup

Using **FILE – PAGE SETUP**, change the margins by clicking the appropriate box and editing the default setting. You can select the orientation of the page, the printer and the paper size. The **PRINT HEADINGS** check box, if not checked, will suppress the printing of the field names as headings.

45

Deleting a query

Once a query has been created, it is usually saved unless it is an 'ad hoc' query providing an answer to a question that is not likely to be asked again. As database application evolves, some queries may outlive their usefulness or be superseded and need to be removed.

Before deleting a query it is important to check that no forms or reports are based on it. We will see how to do this later, so it is important to assign any associated forms or reports to alternative queries or to delete them as well. At present there is nothing based on the queries we have created and they may be deleted safely:

1 To delete a query, from the database window, click on the **QUERIES** object type to display the queries.

2 Highlight the query created by the wizard, (**Dates of Joining**) and press **DELETE**.

3 Reply **YES** to confirm the delete operation.

Data selection – query criteria

Topic objectives

The reasons for devising queries are many and various and are to serve the purpose of the database. To devise queries, criteria need to be set, and these criteria are entered into the criteria cells of the **QUERY** design grid. Querying is done by example, so an example of the answer to the question is entered into the criteria cells.

This topic will show you how to:

- specify query criteria
- rename and hide fields in a query
- use logic in queries.

In business, queries are important in decision-making. To be able to question data relating to, for example, marketing or management, can be very effective using a database management system. In the case of Total Health and Fitness, answers to questions could help with decisions regarding:

- The localities from which the clientele is drawn.
- Provision of smoking and non-smoking areas.
- Introduction of activities and facilities for business clients.
- Introduction of a discount scheme for loyal clients.
- Fees charged for various membership status types.

Using query by example

By creating an example of the values to enable specific records to be retrieved from the database, the enquirer is able to construct queries. For example:

- Which clients live in Harrogate?
- Which clients are non-smokers?
- Which clients are under 25?
- Which clients have been members for more than two years?
- Which clients are family members (i.e. status 3 and 4)?

The values entered in the query grid are called query criteria and we shall now see how to use query criteria to answer the questions posed above, using the **Client** table. Fields of datatype text, number, date and yes/no will be used.

1 Create a new query using the **Client** table and add all the fields to the query (refer back to the previous topic).

Which members live in Harrogate?

2 In the criteria cell of the **Town** field key in ***Harrogate***

3 Click on the **Run** button and the resulting dynaset should only contain records for which the **Town** field is equal to Harrogate.

| Town |
| Client |
| |
| ☑ |
| Harrogate |

4 Click on the **DESIGN VIEW** button to return to the Query Design view. You will see that Access has put double quotes around Harrogate. Access does this when it recognises your criterion as text.

5 Delete the criterion **"Harrogate"** by double-clicking on the word and pressing | **DELETE**. Alternatively, point to just inside the left edge of the cell. The point changes to a right-pointing arrow. Click to select the cell contents and press | **DELETE** to remove the criterion.

6 In the criteria cell of the **Smoker** field, select **NO**. You may need to scroll to the right to display this cell on the screen.

Which clients are non-smokers?

Smoker
Client
☑
No

7 Click on the **RUN** button and view the resulting dynaset. Return to the Design view. Delete the last criterion.

8 In the criteria cell of the **Date of Birth** field, key in **>1/1/75**

9 Click on the **RUN** button and view the resulting dynaset. Return to the Design view. Notice that Access has recognised your query example as a date and converted it to **>#01/01/75#**

Which clients are under 25?

Date of birth
Client
☑
>#01/01/75#

10 Delete this criterion.

11 In the criteria cell of the **Date of Joining**, field key in **<1/1/98**

Which clients have been members for more than two years?

Date of joining
Client
☑
>#01/01/98#

12 Click on the **RUN** button and view the resulting dynaset. Return to the Design view. Delete this criterion.

13 In the criteria cell of the **Status** field, key in **>=5**

14 Click on the **RUN** button and view the resulting dynaset.

15 Return to the Design view.

16 Close the query without saving it.

Which clients are business or social members (i.e. status 5 and 6)?

Status
Client
☑
>=5

47

Query display – renaming fields

When queries are displayed it is sometimes necessary to widen the column so that the field name at the top of the column can be seen. This in turn can lead to unnecessarily wide columns, so it is useful to be able to rename the field. The field header can be renamed in a query with an alternative name. For example, **Joined** instead of **Date of Joining**.

Note: Renaming the field header does not affect the field name in the underlying table.

1 Create a new query using the **Client** table using design view.

2 Add the following fields: **Client No, Title, Last Name, Street, Town, County, Post Code** and, **Date of Joining**.

③ Point to the beginning of the field header **Date of Joining** and click. The aim is to put the flashing insertion point at the beginning of the header name. If you accidentally select the header, press F2 to deselect it. If the insertion point is not at the beginning, press the HOME key to move it to the first character position.

Joined: Date of joining	▼
Client	
☑	

④ Type in the new name for the field, and follow the name with a colon. Do not put a space between the name and the colon. The colon separates the name you key in from the existing field name, which moves to the right to make room for your addition.

⑤ Click on the **RUN** button and the query result with amended field header will be displayed. Return to Design view and set the **SORT** cell for **Joined** to ascending and view the result in date of joining order. Save the query as **Dates of Joining**.

Joined: Date of joining
Client
Ascending
☑

Query display – hiding fields

You have seen how to select the fields you want to see in the result of a query and how to impose criteria. The resulting dynaset displays only the records that match the criteria and shows only the fields specified in the query. To be able to set a criterion on a field, that field needs to be in the query grid and, by default, it will appear in the dynaset. This may not always be desirable, so Access offers the choice of whether or not the field forms part of the dynaset. To prevent a field being displayed in the dynaset yet use a criterion on that field, remove the tick from the box in the **SHOW** cell.

If you wish to select all female clients, it is not necessary to see the gender field in the dynaset display:

① Create a new query using the **Client** table. Add the following fields to the query: **Status, First Name, Last Name, Profession** and **Gender**.

② In the criteria cell of the **Gender** field key in **NO**. Click on the tick box in the Show cell of the **Gender** field to remove the tick and hence hide this field.

③ Set the **SORT** cell to **ASCENDING** for **Last Name**.

④ Click on the **RUN QUERY** button to view the result of the query. The **Gender** field should not form part of the dynaset display, although it has been instrumental in its creation.

⑤ Save the query as **Professions of Female Clients**.

Combining several criteria using AND

① Create a new query using the **Client** table. Add the following fields to the query: **Status, First Name, Last Name, Street, Town, County, Post Code, Smoker** and **Gender**.

2 You can use a criterion in more than one field in a query. Here we will select the male smokers. In the criteria cell for **Gender** key in **YES** and in **Smoker** key in **YES**. The question we have just created is 'Is the client male AND does he smoke?' There is a logical AND between the two criteria; both criteria must be true for the record to be retrieved.

3 Sort on the **Last Name** field and display the dynaset.

4 Return to Design view and save this query as **Addresses of Male Smokers**. Close the query.

5 Create a new query using the **Client** table. Add the following fields: **Title, First Name, Last Name, Telephone No** and **Date of Joining**.

6 Rather than specifying a single criterion for a field several criteria can be specified (for example, clients who joined in a certain time period). The question is 'Who joined between 1/1/99 and 1/1/00?' This is two criteria (i.e. select clients whose date of joining was after 1/1/99 AND before the 1/1/00).

7 In the criteria cell the word 'and' is used between the two criteria. Key in *>=1/1/99* and *< 1/1/00* in the criteria cell of **Date of Joining**. Note that Access will convert this to read *>=#01/01/99#* **AND** *<#01/01/00#*.

8 Rename the **Date of Joining** field as **Joined**. Sort the **Joined** field in descending order.

9 Display and print the dynaset. Save the query giving it the name **Joined 1999** and close the query.

More than two criteria may be specified but remember to put the word AND between them. The following table summarises the mathematical operators that can be used in query criteria:

Mathematical operator	Meaning
<	less than
>	greater than
<>	not equal to
>=	greater than or equal to
<=	less than or equal to
+	addition
–	subtraction
*	multiplication
/	division

Combining several criteria using OR

The other form of logic that is used in queries is OR. There is a row entitled **OR:** in the query design grid. We have already seen OR in action using a filter.

The following query lists the names of the clients who are likely to use the Fitness Floor as their interests are body pump, aerobics (low or high impact), or yoga.

1 Create a new query using the **Client** table.

2 Add the following fields **Client No, Status, Last Name, Town** and **Fitness Interests**

3 In the criteria field of **Fitness Interests** key in
"*body pump*" This criterion asks Access to look for the words 'body pump' anywhere in the data entered in that field. Note that Access will convert this to read **Like "*BODY PUMP*"**.

4 In the **OR:** field of **Fitness Interests** key in **"*aerobics*"**

5 In the row below key in **"*yoga*"**

6 Hide the **Fitness Interests** field.

7 Sort the **Last Name** field in ascending order.

8 Display the dynaset. Notice that when querying text Access is not case-sensitive, **"*yoga*"** will find yoga, YOGA or Yoga.

9 Save this query as **Fitness Floor Usage**. Print the dynaset.

Fitness Interests	
Client	
	☑
Like "*body pump*"	
Like "*aerobics*"	
Like "*yoga*"	

The following table summarises the text operators that can be used in query criteria:

Text operators

"R*"	text strings beginning with R
"*Borough"	text strings ending with borough
"*C*"	text strings containing the letter c

50

More practice with query criteria

Create queries to answer each of the following questions. Examine the dynaset created. Hide any fields that should not be shown, either because they are irrelevant or because the same value is held by all records in the dynaset. Save each of the queries in turn, under a name of your choice.

1 Which clients do not live in Harrogate? Show the following fields for records in the dynaset: **Title, First Name, Last Name, Street** and **Town**.

2 Which clients are female? Display the following fields: **Last Name, First Name** and **Telephone No**.

3 Which clients joined before 1/1/00? Display: **Title, Last Name, First Name** and **Date of Joining**.

4 Which clients have expressed an interest in Fit Kids?

The following queries require the use of the logical query operators, AND and OR. Create queries that show all the fields in the record in answer to the following questions:

1 Which clients have fitness interests that are either swimming or aqua aerobics? This provides a perspective on pool usage.

2 Which clients joined in 2000?

3 Which clients are from Harrogate and are interested in weight management?

(4) Which clients have family status (3 or 4), and what are their dates of joining?

Editing and renaming a query

Once a query has been saved it can be used again and again. More records may be added to the table and each time a query is used, it uses the data currently held in the table. However, as a database develops, a query may be changed to accommodate changing requirements. If the query is modified it may be advisable to change its name so that it remains as meaningful as possible.

(1) Open the query **Fitness Floor Usage**. Edit this query to find clients who express an interest in aerobics, but not aqua aerobics, by removing the previous criteria and in the Fitness Interests field, using the criterion *"*aerobics*" and not "*aqua*"'*.

(2) Save the query. In the database window, select this query and choose **EDIT – RENAME**. Give the query the new name of **Aerobics**.

Note: You could create two queries by using **FILE – SAVE AS** when the **Fitness Floor Usage** query is open or selected in the database window so as to preserve it and to name the new query **Aerobics** (Figure 9.1).

FIGURE 9.1

51

Calculations in queries

Topic objectives

In addition to selecting data, queries can perform calculations on the data selected. There are many occasions when it is useful to count the number of records selected, to add up or take the average of certain fields or to create new fields by calculation. Here we briefly explain some of the basic concepts and give a few examples.

This topic will show you how to:

- create new fields by calculation
- count and average fields, and group and average fields
- use criteria in a summary query.

Creating a new field by calculation

A new field can be created from a calculation using existing fields in the table. For example, if there is a price field which does not include sales tax, a sales tax field can be calculated by multiplying the price by the rate of the tax. In our database application we shall use a calculated field to work out client ages. Why is this better than just recording the client's age directly?

1 Create a new query using the **Client** table.

2 Add the fields **Date of Birth** and **Last Name**.

3 To create a calculated field, in the next empty field cell enter an expression to calculate the new field. The expression takes the form **NAME OF CALCULATED FIELD:EXPRESSION**. Click in the next field cell and create a calculated field by keying in **Age:Year(Now())-Year([Date of Birth])**

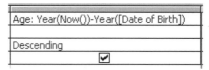

| Age: Year(Now())-Year([Date of Birth]) |
| Descending |
| ☑ |

4 Sort the **Age** field in descending order. Run the query to display the data on screen and print the resulting dynaset.

5 Save the query with the name **Client Ages**.

Expressions used in a calculated field recognise other fields as they are written enclosed in square brackets. For example, VAT: [Cost]*0.175 or Total price: [Price]*[Quantity]

Expressions may be used with date data types, and there are several date functions available. Those you might find useful are described below:

- Year(), which returns the year of the date/time value enclosed in brackets as an integer number (for example, Year([Date of Joining]) might result in 2002).

- Month( ), which returns the month number of the date/time value enclosed in brackets as an integer number (for example, Month([Date of Joining]) might result in 6 (for June).
- Day( ), which returns the day number of the date/time value enclosed in brackets as an integer number (for example Day([Date of Joining]) might result in 22).
- Weekday(date, return type), which returns the day of the week of the date/time value enclosed in brackets as an integer number (for example Weekday([Date of Joining],1) might result in 2 (Tuesday)). The **RETURN TYPE** is a number where 1 indicates Sunday = 1 to Saturday = 7, 2 indicates Monday = 1 to Sunday = 7, and 3 indicates Tuesday = 1 to Monday = 7, etc.
- Now( ), which returns the date and time of the computer's system clock.

Counting and averaging fields

1 Open the query **Client Ages** in design view. Click on the **TOTALS** Σ button to display the **TOTAL:** row.

2 Open the **TOTAL** cell drop-down list. For the **Last Name** and **Date of Birth** fields select **COUNT**.

3 In the total cell for the **Age** field select **AVG** (average). Right click on the **Age** column in the grid and choose **PROPERTIES** from the shortcut menu. Under **FORMAT** select **FIXED** to give two places of decimals.

Field:	Last Name	Date of birth	Age: ((Year(Now())-Year([Date of Birth])))
Table:	Client	Client	
Total:	Count	Count	Avg
Sort:			
Show:	☑	☑	☑
Criteria:			

4 Run the query. The result of this query is different from the normal dynaset display. Only one row is displayed, which contains summary information according to the specification in the **TOTAL** row. Returning to the Design view and clicking on the **TOTALS** button will cause the **TOTAL** row to disappear, and the query reverts to its original 'select' form.

CountOfLast Name	CountOfDate of birth	Age
20	19	33.16

If you save the summary form of this query, and close it, when you open it again, notice that Access will have changed the calculated field to **AGE:AVG(YEAR(NOW())-YEAR([DATE OF BIRTH]))** and put **EXPRESSION** in the **TOTAL** row.

Why is **CountOfLast Name** different from **CountOfDate of Birth**? Refer back to the section on null values in Topic 5.

Summary functions available in queries

Each cell in the **TOTAL:** row has its own drop-down list. Various statistical functions are available:

Function	Purpose
COUNT	Results in the number of records
SUM	Results in a total of all values in that particular field
MIN, MAX	Results in the maximum or minimum value of that particular field
AVG, STDEV, VAR	Results in the average, standard deviation or variance of a particular field
GROUP BY	Groups records according to this field, producing summary statistics for each group
WHERE	Allows criteria to be specified

(Field: Membership No / Table: Membership / Total: Group By / Sort: Group By / Show: Sum / Criteria: Avg / or: Min / Max / Count / StDev / Var)

Totals (such as the total number of sales in the past month) and averages (such as the average number of ticket sales per day) are examples of useful business information. Summary statistics may be calculated for all the records in the table or just for the ones selected by the query.

Grouping and averaging fields

1 Working with the query **Client Ages**, add the **Status** field to the query.

2 In the **TOTAL** cell for the **Status** field, select **GROUP BY** and choose **ASCENDING** as the sort order for this field.

Field:	Status	Last Name	Date of birth	Age: Avg((Year(Now())-Year([Date of Birth])))
Table:	Client	Client	Client	
Total:	Group By	Count	Count	Expression
Sort:	Ascending			
Show:	☑	☑	☑	☑

3 Run the query. The result is displayed as a row for each status and the average age of clients in each status band is calculated.

Status	CountOfLast Name	CountOfDate of birth	Age
1	6	6	35.5
2	2	2	40
3	3	3	40
4	3	3	12
5	4	3	44
6	2	2	24.5

Using criteria in a summary query

1 Continuing to work with the **Client Ages** query, return to Design view. In the Total cell for the **Status** field select **WHERE**.

2 In the **CRITERIA** row put *1 OR 2* (this is equivalent to putting 1 in the **CRITERIA** row and 2 in the **OR** row).

3 Remove the sort order from **Status**.

4 Hide the **Status** field.

Field:	Status	Last Name	Date of birth	Age: Avg((Year(Now())-Year([Date of Birth])))
Table:	Client	Client	Client	
Total:	Where	Count	Count	Expression
Sort:				
Show:	☐	☑	☑	☑
Criteria:	1 Or 2			

5 Run the query. The result should be the total number of clients belonging to status 1 and 2 and their average age.

CountOfLast Name	CountOfDate of birth	Age
8	8	36.625

6 Try this for clients belonging to status 5 or 6. Save the query.

7 Rename this query as **Average Ages**. With **Client Ages** selected in the database window, choose **EDIT – RENAME** and change the name to **Average Ages**.

Refining date calculations

The previous calculation of a client's age is somewhat imprecise because only the difference in years between the date of birth and today's date has been calculated. Using the date of joining field, we can explore a more precise calculation of elapsed time.

1 Create a new query using the **Client** table. Add the **Date of Joining** field and create a calculated field **Days elapsed: Now()-[Date of joining]**

2 Run this query and you will see the number of days each client has been a member. Return to Design view and add another calculated field **Years elapsed: [Days elapsed]/365**

3 To be more precise, you could divide by 365.25 to take into account leap years. View the result of this calculated field. To work out the number of whole years a client has been with the health club use the field **Whole years: int([Years elapsed])**

4 To work out how much additional time on top of whole years a client has been enrolled, the whole number of years multiplied by 365 subtracted from the number of days will give a remainder of days. Use the following calculated field **Remainder days: [Days elapsed]-[Whole years]*365**

5 To turn remainder days into months, use **Months elapsed: int([Remainder days]/30)**

6 See if you can continue this calculation to find weeks elapsed left over after months elapsed. It is not necessary to save this query.

Access also provides a date difference function. **DATEDIFF("YYYY",[DATE OF JOINING],NOW())** will give a year difference the same as **YEAR(NOW())-YEAR([DATE OF JOINING])**. This function can be used to find the number of months between two dates. For example, a calculated field **Months elapsed: DateDiff("m",[Date of last renewal],Now())**

55

Screen forms

Topic objectives

When data is collected manually it is often by means of filling out a form. In a form there are boxes to fill in with, for example, name, address, etc., and there may be boxes that are ticked (for example yes/no boxes). Access offers the facility to create a form on the screen so that data can be entered into a table by simply filling in the form. Filling in such a form should be more user-friendly than filling in the cells in a datasheet, provided the form has been designed carefully. Forms can be used to enter, edit, display and print data contained in your tables. They offer the advantage of presenting data, on screen, in an organised and attractive manner.

This topic will show you how to:

- create a form using AutoForm
- create a form using the Form Wizard
- save a form
- use a form
- print a form.

In this topic you will design forms to enter data into the tables in the database. It is usual to have a form for each table of data for the purpose of entering and editing data in that table. A form can be based upon a table or a view created from a query. A query can use more than one table, so the form created from such a query can be used to enter data into several different tables. This will be explored in later topics.

There are three approaches to creating a form in Access:

- using Autoform
- using Form Wizard
- using your own design.

The first two of these are explored in this unit. They are quick and easy. In Topics 12 and 13 you will learn to modify these standard forms and to design a form from its basic components.

FIGURE 11.1

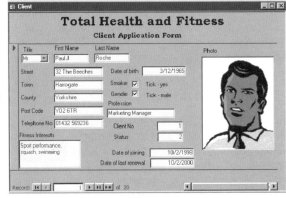

Using AutoForm

AutoForm will create a form instantly using all fields in the records of the underlying table that you choose to base your form upon.

In this task a single-column **Client** form will be created which can later be modified to look like the form shown in Figure 11.1. The order in which the fields are selected for the form is important, as will become apparent when the form is used to enter data. To create this form:

1 From the database window, click on the **FORMS** object type and click on the **NEW** button. Or click on the **NEW OBJECT** 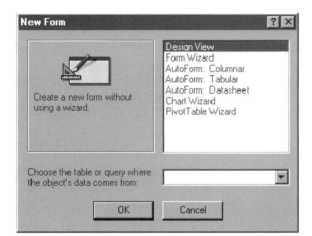 button in the toolbar and select **FORM**. A **NEW FORM** dialog box appears (Figure 11.2).

FIGURE 11.2

57

2 Display the list of tables in the **NEW FORM** dialog box and select **Client** from the list of tables. Select **AUTOFORM: COLUMNAR** and click on **OK**.

3 Access creates a form with a title and a list of field names in a column with a corresponding list of data for the first record in another column. Notice there are some differences between this form and the one shown in Figure 11.1. Customising the form will be considered in Topic 12.

4 Choose **FILE – SAVE** or click on the **SAVE** button and give the form the name **Client**.

5 Close the form, using **FILE – CLOSE** or the **CLOSE** button of the form window. If the form or the latest modification has not been saved, you will be prompted to save. When a form is closed, its name (the one you gave to it when saving) will be shown in the database window when the **FORMS** object type is selected. Clicking on this will open the form again.

Form titles, names and types

Remember, there is a distinction between the name and the title of a form. The title is displayed at the top of the form window. The name you give when saving the form is the form's filename, which you need to be able to recognise when you want to open the form for use again. These names appear in the database window when the **FORMS** object type is selected.

You have just created a columnar form. There are three types of form that can be created using AutoForm: columnar, tabular and datasheet. A columnar form will display data from one record at a time, allowing the user to input one record at a time. The form shown in Figure 11.1 started as a columnar form, but has been modified slightly. Tabular and datasheet forms are very similar in that they display more than one record at one. Due to the tabular format, if there are lots of fields in the records, then an entire record will not fit on one screen.

Using Form Wizard

In this task we will experiment with using the Form Wizard. The Form Wizard will be used to create a tabular form. Remember that, in a tabular form, the number of records displayed will depend upon the size of the window and the number of records in the table. If there are a lot of fields in a record is unlikely you will be able to see the complete record on the screen and you will need to scroll to the right to display more of the fields. This type of form is suited to records with a few fields only, such as those in the **Client Status** table.

No data has been entered into the **Client Status** table. This task will create a form that can later be used for this purpose.

1 First, close any open form. Check that, in the database window, the **FORMS** object type is selected.

2 Either double-click on **CREATE FORM BY USING WIZARD** or click on **NEW**, select **FORM WIZARD** and click on **OK**. The **FORM WIZARD** dialog box is displayed.

3 In the **TABLES/QUERIES** drop-down box, select the **Client Status** table.

4 Add all the fields to the form and click on the **NEXT>** button (see below for additional information).

5 Choose a **TABULAR** form.

6 You are then asked what kind of style you want for your form and are given a choice of various styles. An example of the style is shown to the left of the dialog box. Click on each style in turn to see what it would look like. For this task choose the style called **STANDARD.**

7 Give the form the title **Client Status**.

8 Click on the **FINISH** button to display the form.

9 Save the form as **Client Status** by choosing **FILE – SAVE AS**, or by clicking on the **SAVE** button.

10 Close the form.

Adding fields to forms with Form Wizard

The fields you can have in the form are shown in the **AVAILABLE FIELDS** box.

These can be transferred to the **FIELD ORDER ON FORM** box by means of selecting each field in turn and clicking on the ⟩ button. If you wish to add all the fields in the table to the form, click on the ⟩⟩ button. You may set the order in which the fields appear on the form by selecting them in the order you desire. The ⟨ button will remove a highlighted field from a form and ⟨⟨ will remove all the fields from the form.

Once you have added the required fields to the form continue by clicking on the **NEXT>** button. Key an appropriate title for your form in to the text box. Now click on the **FINISH** button to display the form with data in it.

To open a form from the database window, select the **FORMS** object type, highlight the name of the form required and click on the **OPEN** [Open] button.

Using a form

You can use the form to look at the data in the table (or query) upon which it is based. Whether it is a single column or tabular form, use the record movement keys in the status bar or use the **EDIT – GOTO** menu to move around the records in your form. Using the **PAGE UP** and **PAGE DOWN** keys with a single column form will display the next/previous record whereas, with a tabular form, they will either page up or down a screen of records.

To use the **Client Status** form to enter data into the client status table:

1. Display the available forms in the database window by clicking on the **FORMS** object type in that window. Open the form by either selecting it and clicking on **OPEN**, or by double-clicking on its name.

2. Go to the end of your records using the **NEW RECORD** button on the status bar. If your form is single column, press the **PAGE DOWN** key and a blank form appears. If your form is tabular, click in the first field of the blank record shown at the end of your records.

3. Enter data for another record by filling in the boxes for each field. When you have completed each text box (control) press **ENTER** or **TAB** to move to the next one. Enter data as shown in Figure 11.3 As you enter each record it is saved to the **Client Status** table.

4. Close the form.

59

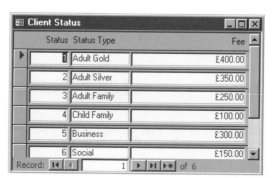

FIGURE 11.3

Printing a form

The primary function of a form is for data to be entered via the computer and display the data on screen). Printing data is usually achieved using a report, however, Access offers the facility to print from a form. Before printing a form always preview it first. A form can be previewed from either the Run or Design view mode.

Previewing before printing

Previewing will display a miniature version of what is to be printed. This allows the layout to be assessed so that adjustments can be made before printing.

To preview the **Client Status** form:

1 Open the **Client Status** form.

2 Click on the **PRINT PREVIEW** button on the toolbar, and a miniature version of what is to be printed will be displayed.

3 To zoom in and zoom out, simply click anywhere on the preview or use the **ZOOM** button. Clicking on the right mouse button will allow you to select the degree of magnification.

4 Choose **FILE – PAGE SETUP** to make adjustments, such as the orientation, portrait or landscape, the choice of printer and the width of the margins. Click on **OK** when the required adjustments have been made.

Printing

Once adjustments have been made in preview, printing may be done from either the preview screen or the form screen.

To print the **Client Status** form from the preview screen:

1 Choose **FILE – PRINT**.

2 Select whether all or certain pages of the form will be printed and the number of copies. Click on **OK**.

3 Close the form.

To print from the form screen, follow the procedure above.

Printing selected records

Printing forms prints all the records so, to print one record:

1 Open the **Client Status** form and display the record to be printed (for example, Client No 5).

2 Select the record using **EDIT – SELECT RECORD** and then choose **FILE –**

PRINT. In the Print dialog box, choose the selected records option. Note that you cannot preview a selection before printing.

Adding client photographs

First you will need to create some image files suitable for use as client photographs. You may have access to a digital camera and software, or you may have access to a scanner and can scan some suitable images. Having created one or two passport-sized images, as there is limited space on the form, store them in the same folder as your database for convenience. Access supports a variety of image formats (ask the Office Assistant for more details), but bitmap images (.bmp) are a good start.

1. Open the **Client** form and display the first record. Click in the space for the photograph. Choose **INSERT-OBJECT**.

2. In the **INSERT OBJECT** dialog box, select the **CREATE FROM FILE** option. Click on the **BROWSE** button and navigate your way to the image file. This should be straightforward if you have stored your image files in the same folder as your database file.

3. Select the required file and click on **OK**. The image should appear in the designated space on the form. If the image is not satisfactory, you can right click on it and edit or resize it using Microsoft Photo Editor.

4. Move to the next record and repeat this process finding the image file you want for this record.

Customising forms

Topic objectives

AutoForm and Form Wizard manage the form creation process for you. Forms are actually composed of a collection of individual design elements, which are called *controls*. The controls that appear on the forms created so far are:

- labels, so that you know what each part of the form is for
- text boxes, for entering data.

There are other controls, which will be introduced in Topic 18.

This topic will show you how to:

- display the customising tools (toolbox, palette, properties and field list)
- move and size controls
- align controls
- add text to a form
- add the date
- add headers and footers to a printed form.

Customising a form in Form Design view

Although **AUTOFORM** or **FORM WIZARD** are quick ways to create a form, the resulting form is rather standardised in terms of vertical spacing between controls, fonts and colours, so you are likely to want to make modifications. A form may be modified so it is easier for inexperienced users to enter information into the database.

In the previous topic a form was opened in 'form run' or Data view only, the view in which it is possible to enter data. In order to make modifications to a form's layout, a form must be opened in Design view. A form has a different appearance in Design view as illustrated in Figure 12.1 (see 'Form Components'). The aim is to create the form shown in Figure 12.1.

1 To open the **Client** form in design view, from the database window, choose the **FORMS** object type, select **Client** and click on the **DESIGN** button. In Design view you can display the Ruler and Grid to help you position the controls on the form (see 'Using the ruler and the grid').

2 Before you can move or size a control you must select it first. A control is selected by clicking anywhere on its

surface. When selected, the control is enclosed by an outlining rectangle with an anchor rectangle at its upper left corner and five smaller rectangles. These smaller rectangles are sizing handles. On columnar forms, such as this one, text boxes often have associated labels and, when you select one of these objects, they are both selected together as a unit. Select the **Client No** control (see 'Selecting and moving groups of controls').

3 If after selecting, without releasing the mouse button, you begin to drag, the control will move. Otherwise, move the pointer over the selected control until it changes shape to a hand. Click and drag label and control to new position. Move the **Client No** control to a lower central position on the form. You may find it useful to widen the form temporarily so that controls can be moved to temporary positions while you rearrange them on the form (see 'Changing the form's area').

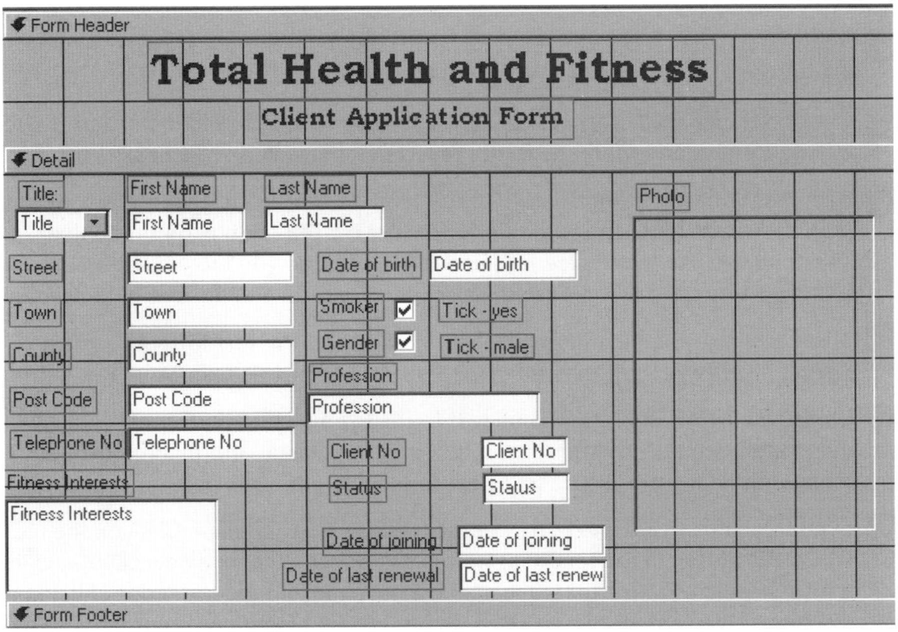

FIGURE 12.1

4 To move a control separately from its label (or vice versa), select the **Fitness Interests** control and move the pointer over the anchor handle at the top left corner of the control. The pointer should change shape to a pointing hand. Click and drag underneath the label.

5 You can select and move more than one control at a time. This is useful if you want to keep the relative spacing of a group of objects yet want to move them to another part of the form. There are two ways of selecting a group of controls (see 'Selecting and moving groups of controls'). Select the **Date of Joining** and **Date of Last Renewal** fields and move them under **Client No.**

6 Once you start to move controls around the form they can become misaligned. By selecting a group of controls together they can be aligned. Select labels and text boxes separately for alignment purposes. Select the **Date of Joining** and **Date of Last Renewal** labels, choose **FORMAT – ALIGN** and, as these are labels, select **RIGHT**. The selected group of controls should all align to the right.

7 Now select the text boxes of these two controls. Choose **FORMAT – ALIGN** and as these are text boxes, select **LEFT**. Continue to work on rearranging the layout so that it is similar to that illustrated. Click on the **SAVE** button at regular intervals to save the form.

8 To see how the form looks for data entry, switch to Form view using **VIEW –**

DESIGN VIEW or clicking on the **VIEW** button. Whilst working on a form's design it is useful to switch between **VIEW** and **DESIGN** using the buttons on the toolbar, or by using **VIEW – FORM VIEW** or **VIEW – DESIGN VIEW**:

View ▣▾   Design ▨▾

9 If you inadvertently delete a field, refer to 'Deleting or restoring fields from or to a form' later in this topic to see how to restore it.

10 Additional text can be added to a form. To add text to the header section of the **Client** form, widen the **FORM HEADER** section.

11 Click on the **LABEL** ▨ tool in the toolbox window. Click in the space created for the form header and key in the text *Total Health and Fitness* .

12 Select and drag a sizing handle of the label to enlarge it. Select the font and size of the text by opening the **FONT/POINT SIZE** list box on the toolbar and selecting the font/point size required. Note that, as you increase the size of a font, you may need to increase the size of the control and the size of the section.

13 Move and size the heading as in Figure 12.1, add the text *Client Application Form* . If you wish you may alter the font or size of this text. Save the form.

14 Using the **LABEL** tool, add some text to the form next to the **Gender** tick box to inform the user of the form that a tick indicates male and blank indicates female. Similarly add some text next to the **Smoker** tick box.

15 Switch to form **VIEW** ▶∗ to try out the form by entering data. Click on the **NEW RECORD** button in the record selectors. Compose data for a new client and key it into the form. Notice that, because we have rearranged the order of fields on the form, known as the 'Tab Order', the movement from one control to the next does not flow and appears to jump around the form.

16 To alter the Tab Order return to form **DESIGN**, choose **VIEW – TAB ORDER** to display the **TAB ORDER** dialog box (see 'Reorganising the tab order'). Click on the **AUTO ORDER** button and click on **OK**.

17 Try using the form again to enter another record, and note the difference. If you prefer set a custom Tab Order. Save and close the form.

Form headers and footers

Form headers and footers are always displayed on the screen. They can show a company name or logo as well as any titles and labels. Calculated text may be added to the header or the footer. For example, the date can be shown:

1 To put the date in the **Client Status** form footer, open this form in Design view.

2 Choose **INSERT – DATE AND TIME**. Select a suitable date format and click on **OK**. The date is automatically inserted into the form header. Drag the control for the date to the form footer. Save the form.

3 Switch to run mode by clicking on the **VIEW** button to see the result. Close the form.

Adding headers and footers to a printed form

When a form is printed, the header is printed at the beginning and the footer is printed at the end of the records. To add a header and footer that print at the top of each page of the **Client** form when printed (see 'Headers and footers'):

1 Open the **Client** form. Click on the **PRINT PREVIEW** button. Close the preview and display the form in design view.

2 Choose **VIEW – PAGE HEADER/FOOTER**. Two extra sections appear, **PAGE HEADER** and **PAGE FOOTER**.

3 Select all the title in the form header and use **EDIT – COPY**. Click on the Page Header bar and use **EDIT – PASTE**. Position the pasted copy.

4 Click on the **PAGE FOOTER** bar and choose **INSERT – PAGE NUMBER**. Choose a suitable format, select the bottom of page option and click on **OK**.

5 Click on **FORM HEADER** bar. Display the properties sheet, click on the **PROPERTIES** button on the toolbar.

6 In the section properties box select the **ALL** tab and click in the **DISPLAY WHEN** box.

7 Open the list and select **SCREEN ONLY** (Figure 12.2)

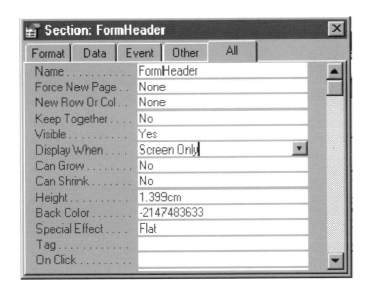

FIGURE 12.2

8 Click on the **DETAIL** bar and change the **KEEP TOGETHER** property to **YES** to prevent page breaks in the middle of records.

9 Preview and print the form. Close the form.

Form components

Component	Description
Form Header	Appears at the top of the form, and can hold information such as the form's title; field labels and graphics
Detail	Contains the controls (field labels, text boxes and check boxes) that display data from your table
Label controls	Contains the field name
Text box controls	The box in which data can be entered or is displayed when the form is run
Form Footer	Appears at the bottom of the form. Similar in function to the Form Header; often contains the date
Scroll Bars	Vertical and horizontal scroll bars enable movement of the form within its window

Selecting and moving groups of controls

To select a group of objects, either:

- Imagine that the group of objects is enclosed by a rectangle (each object need only be partly enclosed by the rectangle). Use the pointer and, by clicking and dragging, draw this rectangle on the form. When you release the mouse button all the objects within this rectangle will be selected. Or
- Select one object and hold down the **SHIFT** key whilst selecting the next and subsequent objects (this is easier when controls are in close proximity).

For example, to select labels for alignment, click on each label while holding down the **SHIFT** key. Alternatively, draw a rectangle that encloses part or all of the labels you wish to select.

To move:

- the whole group – with pointer as the shape of a hand, drag
- an individual control in the group – point to its anchor handle and drag.

To deselect:

- one object in the group – click on it while holding down the **SHIFT** key
- the whole group – click anywhere outside the selected area.

To move the group of objects, click and drag the anchor handle of any of the objects in the group.

Using the ruler and the grid

When a control is being moved, indicator lines move along both rulers to aid positioning of the controls.

If the rulers are not visible use **VIEW – RULER** to display them.

A grid, which is also an aid to the positioning of controls may be displayed or hidden using **VIEW – GRID**. The spacing of the grid can be adjusted by changing the setting of the **GRIDX** and **GRIDY** properties on the form's property sheet. To display the form property sheet use **EDIT – SELECT FORM** and click on the **PROPERTIES** button.

When **FORMAT – SNAP TO GRID** is on (which is indicated by a tick by **SNAP TO GRID** in the menu), any new controls drawn on the form will have their corners aligned to points on the grid. When **SNAP TO GRID** is off the control can be placed anywhere.

Changing the form's area

The area of each section of a form (the header, detail and footer sections) may be altered individually. Also, the position of the right and bottom edge of a form may be adjusted. To alter the depth of a section of the form move the pointer to the bottom edge of the section where it will change shape ↨ . Drag down to increase the depth of the section.

Alter the width of a section by dragging the right and bottom edge to the size you require.

Deleting or restoring fields from or to a form

To delete a label and text box select the control and press **DELETE** or use **EDIT – DELETE** to delete both label and entry box. To delete the label only, click on it again before deleting.

Note: If you delete a field you won't be able to use the form to enter data into this field. Use **EDIT – UNDO** if you unintentionally delete a field.

To restore a label and field use **VIEW – FIELD LIST** to display the list of fields available in the table. Click on the field name required and drag to required position on the form. If the form is a single-column form, both label and field will appear, although the label will require editing. If the form is a tabular one, just the field will be restored.

Editing and sizing controls and labels

The text of a field name label may be edited and, if required, additional text can be added to the form. To edit a label, double-click on the label to display an insertion point in the text. Edit the text as required. Press **ENTER** or click on a blank part of the form when finished.

To adjust the width and height of a control simultaneously, point to one of the small sizing handles at one of the three corners. It should change to a diagonal two-headed arrow. Click and drag to size required.

To adjust the height (width) of a control only, point to one of the sizing handles on the horizontal (vertical) edge of the selection outline so that it is a vertical (horizontal) two-headed arrow. Click and drag to height (width) required.

67

Reorganising the tab order

As data is entered into each field, **ENTER** or **TAB** takes you to the next field. The order in which data is entered into the fields is defined by the order in which they were selected in the **FORM WIZARD**. If a form has been modified, the default order may no longer be appropriate.

FIGURE 12.3

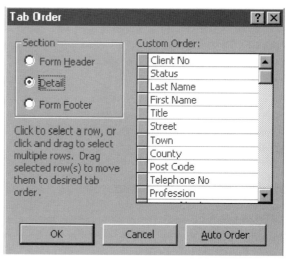

To change the tab order of the fields from the design view, choose **VIEW – TAB ORDER** to display the **TAB ORDER** dialog box (Figure 12.3). This dialog box displays the order of the fields in the **CUSTOM ORDER** box. In the **SECTION** box, normally the detail section is selected.

To alter the order of the fields, select the field or fields to be moved and drag to the new position to achieve the new order. When the new order has been selected, click on **OK**. The **AUTO ORDER** button will set the tab order according to the way in which the fields are set out on the form, and they are ordered with the priority of left to right and then top to bottom.

Headers and footers

If a form is to be printed, the header section prints before the first record and the footer section prints after the last record. Page header and page footer sections can be added which will print on each page of the printout. You can control whether to display or print these sections. A calculated control may be added to show the page numbers. Page breaks may occur in the middle of records (if the record is in single-column format). This can be avoided by adjusting the **KEEP TOGETHER** setting of the **DETAIL** properties from **NO** to **YES**. To display the properties sheet, check the **PROPERTIES** button is depressed and click on the detail bar.

Designing your own forms

Topic objectives

Topics 11 and 12 have introduced creating forms using the Form Wizard. The other route is to create your own forms without first creating a standard form.

This topic will show you how to design your own form, including:

- opening a blank form in Design view
- selecting a form type
- adding controls, such as labels and text boxes to a blank form.

Creating your own form

If the layout and designs available through Form Wizard are not suitable, you need to create a blank form and add and format controls. The first step is to choose the type of form. This task will explore using a blank form that will duplicate one of the forms already created. The table that is to be used is the **Clients** table. You may find it useful to refer to the notes below on adding labels, and adding text boxes, to forms:

1 Select the **FORMS** object type in the database window. Click on **NEW**. In the **NEW FORM** dialog box, click on **DESIGN VIEW**. Choose **Client** as the table. Click on **OK**.

2 Access creates a new form, showing the detail section.

3 Add a header and footer section by choosing **VIEW – FORM HEADER/ FOOTER**.

You should see a matrix of lines on the form's workspace. If not, select **VIEW – GRID** to display it.

4 Adjust the depth of the detail section by pointing to the top line of the Form Footer bar.

The pointer should change shape to a horizontal bar with double-headed arrow. Click and drag downward to expand the detail section area.

5 Add all the fields by clicking and dragging from the field list. Consider the order in which you select and place them. Try selecting and placing a group of fields.

6 Add a title to the form and save the form as **Client2**. (Remember, there is a distinction between the title of the form and the name it is saved under.)

7 Run the form and use it to add another record to the **Client** table.

8 If the order of field entry does not match the form design, for instance, if the fields were not selected in the right order, the order can be changed by returning to Design view and choosing **VIEW – TAB ORDER**. Save the changes.

Choosing the type of form

If a form is created using AutoForm or the Form Wizard, you are given the choice of the type of form. With a blank form the default type is single form. To select a different type of form:

1 In **DESIGN VIEW,** display the **PROPERTIES** window by choosing **VIEW – PROPERTIES** or by clicking on the properties button on the toolbar. Select the table upon which the form is to be based and click on **OK**.

2 In the **FORM PROPERTIES** sheet, you should see the Default View property set to Single form.

3 If you wish to select a different type of form, click on **DEFAULT VIEW** and choose one of the other options (e.g. Continuous Forms).

Creating some more forms

Use the skills you have developed in this and the previous two topics to create some additional forms, and use those forms to enter data into the tables for which they have been created. You will need these tables and their forms as components in the database application you are building.

There are two other tables that require forms to be designed. These are the **Session** table and the **Reservation** table.

1 Use **AUTOFORM** and **FORM WIZARD** to create columnar forms for both these tables, saving them as **Session** and **Reservation** respectively (Figures 13.1 and 13.2)

70

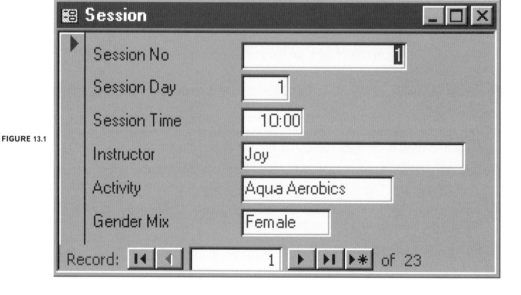

FIGURE 13.1

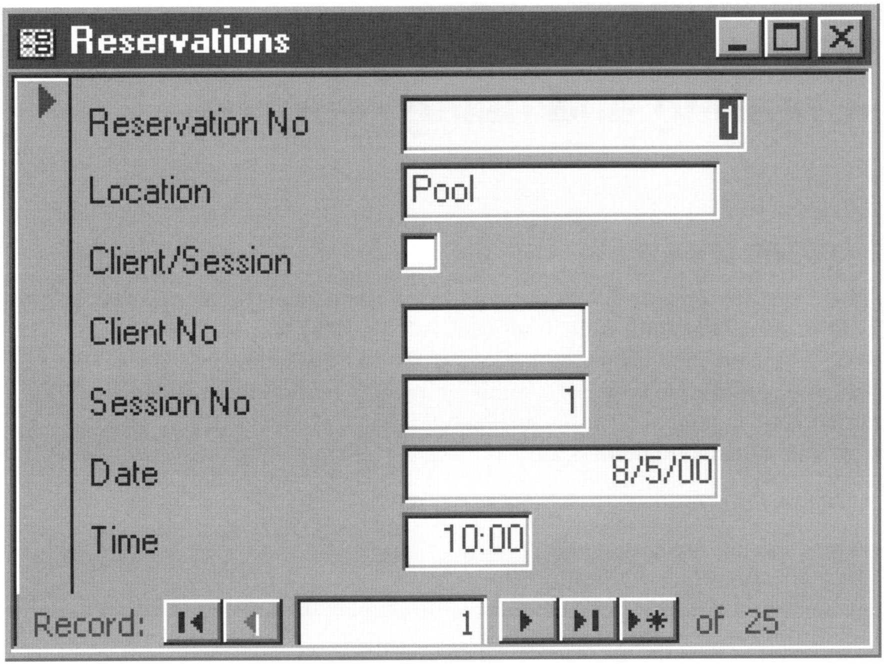

FIGURE 13.2

2️⃣ Use the forms to enter the data for these tables (the data is shown in the Appendix).

Note: Remember that, when entering reservation data, yes (tick) indicates a client and no (blank) indicates a session. Remind yourself of the validation rules set in Topic 4 and try testing them while entering the data.

3️⃣ Close the forms when the data has been entered.

Creating and using reports

Topic objectives

This topic introduces the basic design of printed reports. These reports can be used to display or print selections of the data in an Access table. They are the output forms for data. To remind you of some of the uses of reports, revisit Topic 1. Since various design and creation features are common to reports and forms, you will reuse some of the skills you acquired earlier in designing a form. This topic explains how to create a report quickly using Report Wizard.

This topic will show you how to:

- create a report using AutoReport
- create a report using Report Wizard
- save and close a report
- use a report to print or display data from an Access table.

Creating a tabular report using AutoReport

The really easy way to create a report is to allow Access to do all the work for you by using AutoReport. Whilst AutoReport can be used to create a quick report, there is no scope for specifying the contents or style of the report.

To use AutoReport to create a report for the **Client Status** table:

1. In the database window, select the **REPORTS** object type and click on the **NEW** button.

2. In the **NEW REPORT** dialog box select **AUTOREPORT: TABULAR**.

3. Click on the down arrow button of the **CHOOSE A TABLE OR QUERY...** list box to produce a list of tables and queries. Select the table **Client Status**.

4. Click on **OK** and the report will be created and displayed on the screen, in preview mode.

5. Use **FILE – SAVE** and save the report as **Client Status**.

Using Report Wizard to create a single-column report

Report Wizard helps you to create reports in a number of different formats. First, we create a single-column report which is frequently used and is simple to create. A single-column report places all the selected fields in a single column, with their field names or labels to the left as shown in Figure 14.1.

We wish to create a single-column report that lists the records for all the members who have records in the database, showing the following fields:

Client No
Status
First Name
Last Name
Profession
Date of Birth
Fitness activities.

We wish to create a report that looks like the extract shown in Figure 14.1.

Total Health and Fitness Clients

Client No	1
Status	2
First Name	Paul J
Last Name	Roche
Profession	Marketing Manager
Date of birth	3/12/65
Fitness Interests	Sport performance, squash, swimming

Client No	2
Status	3
First Name	Hilary
Last Name	Price

FIGURE 14.1

73

1. To enter **REPORT WIZARD**, starting from the database window, click on **NEW** in the database window when you are displaying reports, or click the **NEW OBJECT** button on the toolbar and select **REPORT**. A **NEW REPORT** dialog box appears (Figure 14.2).

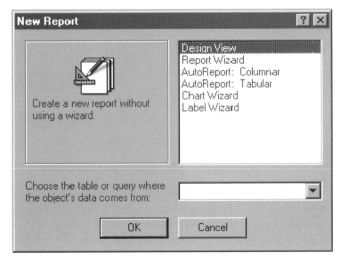

FIGURE 14.2

2 Select the **REPORT WIZARD** option to create a report using Report Wizard.

3 Click on the down arrow button of the **CHOOSE THE TABLE OR QUERY...** list box to produce a list of tables and queries, and select the **Client** table. Click on **OK**.

4 Select the fields to appear in the report by clicking on the field names above in the **AVAILABLE FIELDS** list box, and then clicking on the [>] button. If you wish to add all the fields in the table to the report, click on the [>>] button. You may set the order in which the fields appear on the report by selecting them in the order you desire. The [<] button will remove a highlighted field from a report and [<<] will remove all the fields from the report. The selected fields should appear in the **SELECTED FIELDS** list box. Choose **NEXT>**.

5 The next dialog box asks you to indicate grouping levels. Do not indicate a grouping level. We shall visit grouping levels in Topic 15. If Access has automatically created one (on **Status**), click on [<] to remove the grouping. Click on **NEXT>**.

6 The next dialog box asks you to select the sort order. Choose to sort by **Client No** by selecting it from the first drop-down list box. Click on **NEXT>**.

Note: If you have a small set of records only, just one sort field will be adequate. If you want records to appear in the same order as in the table or query, it is not necessary to indicate a sort field.

7 The next dialog box offers options for the report's layout and orientation. Choose **OUTLINE** 1 and **PORTRAIT** for the layout of the report. Click on **NEXT>**.

8 A range of options for style is offered. The style determines the appearance of field names and field contents in the report. An example of the style is shown on the left of the dialog box. Click on each style in turn to see what it would look like. Choose Corporate for the style of the report. Click on **NEXT>**.

9 Enter the following report title: *Total Health and Fitness Clients* .

Note: Remember that report titles should be informative.

10 With the option **PREVIEW THE REPORT** selected, click on **FINISH** to display the report on the screen. Access has added a page number and the date at the bottom of each page of the report.

11 Access will automatically save the report with the name **Total Health and Fitness Clients**.

Using and printing a report

1 To use and preview the report **Total Health and Fitness Clients**, either:

  ▪ Select it from the filenames displayed in the database window by double clicking on the report name. The Print Preview window will appear showing a preview of how the report will appear when printed. Or

  ▪ Click on the report name and then click on the **PREVIEW** button.

2 To zoom in and zoom out in order to view a complete page on the screen, simply click anywhere on the preview or use the **ZOOM** button. Click on the **ZOOM CONTROL** box to select a specific magnification for the preview.

Note: A report picks up the table properties of the table or query the report uses when it was designed. Later, you will change the properties of the table or query without changing the properties of the report.

Now print the report, thus:

3 Choose **FILE – PAGE SETUP**. Some of the options in the **PAGE SETUP** dialog box will be familiar since you will have used them in printing tables and queries, but there are also special options for use when printing a report, such as the number of columns across the page, and their size.

4 Now experiment with different setup options, for example, experiment with:

  ▪ Two columns across the page by entering 2 in the **NUMBER OF COLUMNS** box. Change the page orientation to landscape and you may need to adjust the **WIDTH** in the **COLUMN SIZE** section to less than half your page width.
  ▪ With 2 columns on the page explore the effect of **DOWN, THEN ACROSS** and **ACROSS, THEN DOWN** in the **COLUMN LAYOUT** section.

Close the **PRINT SETUP** dialog box between each trial in order to view the new layout in Print Preview.

5 When you have a layout with which you are happy, print it by selecting the **PRINT** button, followed by **OK**.

75

Saving and closing a report

Report Wizard automatically saves the reports it creates, but you will want to save, or check you have saved a report if you modify the basic report. Save a report by choosing **FILE – SAVE**. If this is a new report that does not have a name, Access will prompt for a filename with a **FILE – SAVE AS** dialog box. If you later want to save a report under another name, use **FILE – SAVE AS**, and enter the new name in the dialog box.

Remember, there is a distinction between the name and the title of a report. The title is the text that is displayed at the top of the report when it is printed. The name you give when saving the form is the form's filename, which you need to be able to recognise when you want to open the form for use again. These names appear in the database window when the **REPORTS** object type is selected.

Creating and using grouped reports

Topic objectives

This topic explores the creation of grouped report. A grouped report puts the fields you select into a row and groups the records according to the value of a field in the table or query. This approach can also be used simply to create a report in a table form with fields shown in columns (if you do not specify groups). The advantage of this type of report is that it displays more records to the page. However, is does not display records with several long fields that, therefore, cannot be accommodated next to each other on the page in parallel columns.

This topic will show you how to:

▓ create a report with multiple columns
▓ create a report with grouped records.

Note: It is not essential you complete this topic in sequence. You may skip this topic for the moment and return to it later when you are ready to design this kind of report.

Creating a grouped report using Wizard Report

We wish to create a grouped report that lists all the clients for which there are records in the database, showing the following fields for each client:

▓ **Status**
▓ **Last Name**
▓ **First Name**
▓ **Telephone No**.

The records are to be grouped according to **Status** so that, for instance, all records with a given **Status** number are grouped together, as in the report below:

Client list by Status

Status	Last Name	First Name	Telephone No
1			
	Corbett	George	01432 561431
	Evans	Anthony J	01432 567333
	Johnson	Janet E	01432 567822
	Kelly	John D	
	Williams	Ann M	01432 509945
	Woodall	Daniel	
2			
	Mirze	van	01402 561550
	Roche	Paul J	01432 569236

1 Select the **REPORTS** object type and double-click on the **CREATE REPORT BY USING WIZARD** option to create a report using Report Wizard.

2 From the **CHOOSE A TABLE OR QUERY...** drop-down list box, select the **Client** table. Click on **OK**.

3 Select the fields to appear in the report by clicking on the fields names as indicated above, in the **AVAILABLE FIELDS** list box, and then by clicking on the ⟩ button. The selected fields should appear in the **SELECTED FIELDS** list box. If any fields are included by mistake, use ⟨ to remove them.

4 Click on **NEXT>**. You will probably discover that Access has automatically grouped the records by **Status**. If not, click on **Status** in the list of fields and then click on ⟩ to display it in the heading box in the preview (Figure 15.1). Click on **NEXT>**.

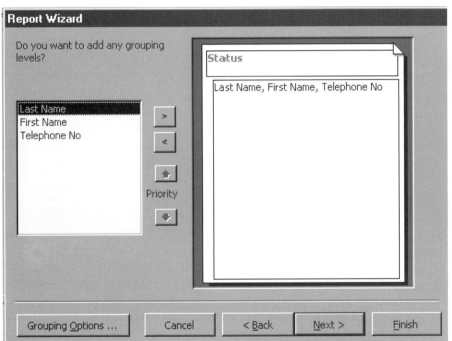

FIGURE 15.1

5 Sort records within groups alphabetically by the **Last Name** field. Choose **NEXT>**.

6 Select **STEPPED** and **PORTRAIT** for the layout of the report. Choose **NEXT>**.

7 Select **COMPACT** for the style of the report. Choose **NEXT>**.

8 Enter the following report title: *Client list by Status*

9 Choose **PREVIEW THE REPORT** and click on **FINISH**. As the Wizard was used to create the report, it is automatically saved with the name of its title (i.e. **Client list by Status**).

10 To print the report directly, click on the **PRINT** button. To change print options display the **PRINT** dialog box using **FILE – PRINT** and make the choices you require before clicking on **OK**.

Creating a grouped report using more than one group

It is possible to use more than one field simultaneously in order to categorise groups in records. In this exercise you will group records by **Status** and **Town**. All records with a given **Status** are grouped together and, within this grouping, all records with a given **Town** will be grouped together. The grouped report will list all the clients for which there are records in the database, showing the following fields:

- **Status**
- **Last Name**
- **First Name**
- **Town**
- **Telephone No**

We wish to create a report that looks like the report shown below:

Client list by Status and Town

Status	Town	Last Name	First Name	Telephone No
	1			
	Harrogate			
		Evans	Anthony J	01432 567333
		Kelly	John D	
		Williams	Ann M	01432 569945
		Woodall	Daniel	
	Knaresborough			
		Corbett	George	01432 551431
		Johnson	Janet E	01432 557822

① Follow the first five steps as for the previous task. You will probably discover that Access has automatically grouped the records by **Status**. If not, click on **Status** in the list of fields and then click on ▸ to display it in the heading box in the preview.

② To add **Town** to the grouping, select it and click on ▸. Click on **NEXT>**.

③ Sort records within groups alphabetically by the **LAST NAME** field (Figure 15.2). Click on **NEXT>**.

④ Select **STEPPED** and **PORTRAIT** for the layout of the report. Click on **NEXT>**.

⑤ Choose **COMPACT** for the style of the report. Click on **NEXT>**.

⑥ Enter the following report title: *Client list by Status and Town*

⑦ Choose **PREVIEW THE REPORT** and click on **FINISH**. As the Report Wizard was used to create the report it is automatically saved with the name of its title (i.e. **Client list by Status and Town**).

⑧ To print the report directly, click on the **PRINT** button. To change print options display the **PRINT** dialog box using **FILE – PRINT** and make the choices you require before clicking on **OK**.

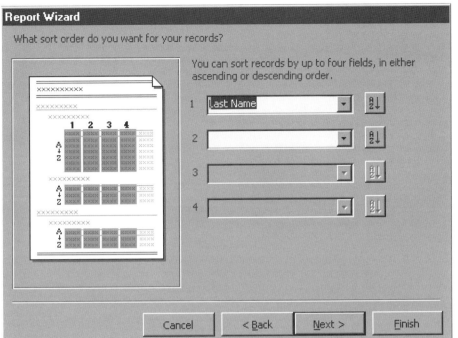

FIGURE 15.2

Selecting the order of grouping

79

1. Create a report that is the same as the one in the previous task, with the records grouped according to **Status** and **Town**. This time show all records with a given **Town** grouped together and, within this grouping, show all records with a given **Status** grouped together.

2. Create this report as in the previous task and, when you have added **Town** as a grouping, click on the **PRIORITY** up arrow to change the priority of grouping.

3. Continue as before but give this report the title *Client list by Town and Status*. Note the difference between this report and the previous one.

TOPIC 16

Mailing label reports and mail merge

Topic objectives

Mailing labels are created using a mailing label report. This type of report can be based on a table or query containing names and address. Field labels do not appear but text characters, such as commas and spaces, can be added easily.

This topic will show you how to:

☐ create a mailing label report
☐ use a query in the process of creating a Report Wizard report
☐ perform a mail merge to create personalised letters to be mailed using the labels.

Creating a mailing label report

The procedure for creating a mailing label report is similar to that for creating any other type of report, except that you use a special Label Wizard.

To create a mailing label report for the **Client** table:

1 With Reports obect type selected in the database window, select **NEW**.

2 Click on the **LABEL WIZARD** option and select the **Clients** table to provide the data for the labels report. Click on **OK** to display the first of the Label Wizard dialogue boxes (Figure 16.1).

FIGURE 16.1

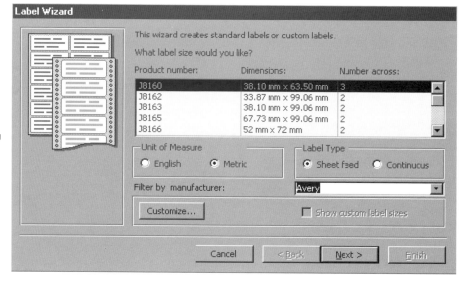

3 Experiment with different label sizes. Select the size of labels from the list. Label sizes are listed according to their Avery number. If you do not know the Avery label number for a given label size, look at the Dimensions and Number

Across column to find the label size that matches your labels. Metric Avery J8160 should be a suitable size.

4 Choose a label type and click on **NEXT>**.

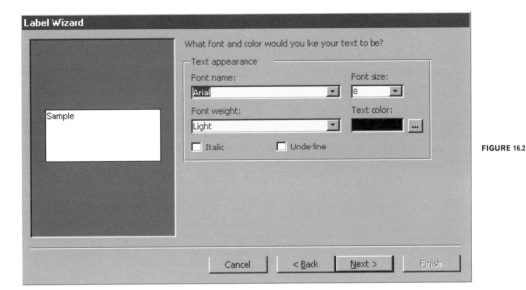

FIGURE 16.2

5 If desired, choose the **FONT NAME**, **FONT SIZE**, **FONT WEIGHT** and **TEXT COLOR**. You may also check **ITALIC** and/or **UNDERLINE**. Click on **NEXT>**.

6 Select the fields to be included (see Figure 16.3). These are, in the order that follows:
Title
Last Name
Street
Town
County
Post Code

7 Add the field **Title** followed by a space and then the field **Last Name** to the first line. Click on the **ENTER** button to move on to the next line.

8 Add **Street** to the next line.

9 Add the remainder of the fields, each to a separate line, with the exception of **County** and **Post Code** which should be on the same line separated by a comma and a space. Click on **NEXT>**.

10 Choose to order the records in alphabetical order according to **Last Name**. Click on **NEXT>**.

11 Accept the title *Labels Client*. The report is automatically saved.

12 With **SEE THE LABELS...** selected, click on **FINISH** to display the report on the screen.

13 To ensure that the post codes are always in upper case, view the report in design view and put > in the **FORMAT** property for the control containing the post code. Preview the labels report.

14 To print the report directly select the **PRINT** button. To display the **PRINT** dialog box use **FILE – PRINT**.

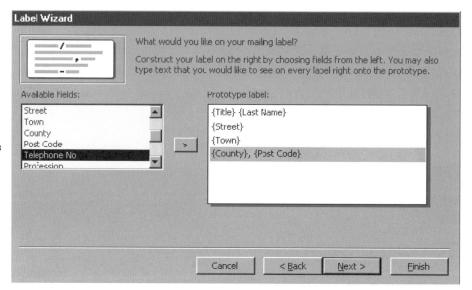

FIGURE 16.3

Creating a mailing label report based on a query

Often, mailing labels are required only for a subset of a database. For example, we may wish to send a notice about our new facilities to selected clients. Here you will create a mailing label report which lists all clients who joined since 1/6/99. Some of the labels from such a report are shown below. First we define and execute a query to select the appropriate records. Next we define the mailing label report that is to be used to create labels from these records:

Mr Butler
6 Park Road
Harrogate
Yorkshire YO1 3RE

Mr Corbett
6 The Square
Knaresborough
Yorkshire YO7 1YJ

Query design and execution were introduced earlier (see Topics 8–9 and 10). This exercise should help you to review this topic at this point.

To define the query:

1 Starting from the database window, select the **QUERIES** object type and click on the **NEW** button to create a new query.

2 The **NEW QUERY** dialog box appears. Choose **DESIGN VIEW**. Click on **OK.**

3 The **SHOW TABLE** dialog box appears. Select the table **Client** and click on the **ADD** button and then click on the **CLOSE** button.

4 Next, choose to include all fields in the query by double-clicking on the title bar of the field list box of the table in the upper section of the window. Click anywhere in the selected area and drag to the field row to transfer all the fields to the lower section.

5 In the **Date of Joining** criteria cell, enter the query criteria *>1/6/99*. To view the result of this query, click on the **RUN** button on the toolbar. Note that, in reality, to create this type of query that could be used regularly it would be better to add a calculated field *Recent: DateDiff("m",[Date of Joining],Now())* and use the criteria *<=6* for the past six months. To try this out, enter some new client records with recent joining dates.

6 Now we will exclude family status clients as we do not want to print a separate label for each family member so, in the **Status** criterion, put *Not (3 Or 4)*. Remember the brackets are important. Why? Family clients can be dealt with on a separate mailing label report.

7 Save the query by choosing **FILE – SAVE**.

8 In the **QUERY NAME** box of the **SAVE AS** dialog box, enter the query name: **New Clients**.

9 Close the query. Now you have defined a query, the mailing labels to print the records retrieved by the query need to be created.

10 Go through the same steps as with the pervious exercise, using the Label Wizard, but, on this occasion from the **CHOOSE A TABLE OR QUERY**... drop-down list box, select the query **New Clients**.

11 Accept the title *Labels New Clients*. The report is automatically saved.

12 View the labels on the screen or print them to check you have completed the exercise successfully.

To create a mailing label report for the family clients (i.e. one label per family), first create a query based on the **Client** table that only selects the family members. Add the fields **Status**, **Last Name**, **Street**, **Town**, **County** and **Post Code** to the query. Set the criterion *3 Or 4* for **Status**. Click on the **TOTALS** button and change **GROUP BY** under **Status** to **WHERE** and hide this field. The result of this query should be one row per family and can be used for a mailing label report in which the first line of the label could read *The {Last Name} Family*

83

Mail merging

As well as creating labels for envelopes a mail shot often involves the production of standard letters. This process is automated by using Access in conjunction with Word to perform a mail merge. Using Word, a letter can be produced and Access can provide the data (usually names and addresses) to be merged with the letter, for personalisation.

Access and Word are required for the following task. A letter will be sent to all the clients of status 1, 2 and 5. Create a query based on the **Client** table using all fields and selecting status 1, 2, and 5. Save this query as **Gold, Silver and Business Clients**.

Merge It with MS Word
Publish It with MS Word
Analyze It with MS Excel

1 With the **QUERIES** object type selected, highlight the **Gold, Silver and Business Clients** query in the database window.

2 Open the **OFFICE LINKS** drop-down list (on the toolbar) and select **MERGE IT WITH MS WORD** (Figure 16.4).

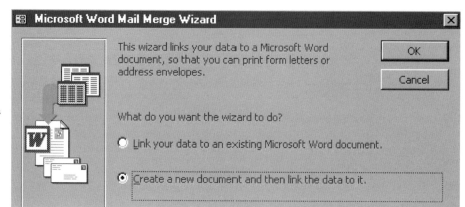

FIGURE 16.4

③ Choose the option to create a new document and click on **OK**. This causes Word to be loaded in mail merge mode. *Note*: Ensure there is data in the object, table or query you have selected, otherwise this will not work.

④ Next create a standard letter as illustrated below. The parts of the letter that are replaceable fields are shown enclosed in double chevrons. To insert a replaceable field, click on the **INSERT MERGE FIELD** button on the mail merge toolbar and select the required field from the drop-down list.

⑤ It is best to check the merge for errors first. Do this by clicking on the **VIEW MERGED DATA**. Check the merged data. Save the document.

⑥ To complete the task, design a mailing label report to accompany the letters produced.

Total Health and Fitness
Manchester Avenue
Harrogate
Yorkshire
YO2 1SJ

Tel: 01432 564344
Fax: 01432 560121

21 May, 200X

< <Street> >
< <Town> >
< <County> >
< <Post Code> >

Dear < <Title> >   < <Last Name> >

As many of you will be aware we have recently completed the renovation and extension of our facilities at Total Health and Fitness. A leaflet describing the enhanced facilities is enclosed, together with two tickets to the official opening of the new suites.

I look forward to sharing this opportunity to celebrate the success and future of Total Health and Fitness with you.

Yours sincerely

R S Shepherd B.A, M.Sc.
Manager

Customising reports

Topic objectives

This topic explores the customisation of reports that have been created with Report Wizards, or new reports created from a blank report. Customisation offers a wider range of options in report designing.

This topic show will you how to:

- understand the component parts of a report
- move and size controls
- change the report's area
- delete, add and restore fields to a report
- change the text of a field name
- add headers and footers.

Working with report design allows you to adjust the contents, size and position of everything that appears on the report. As with forms, each small piece of a report is called a *control*. Controls include a fields data, text, picture and calculations. Again, many of the features relating to forms that you experimented with earlier also apply to reports.

Examining the components of a report

1 Examine one of the reports you have created with Report Wizard in Topic 14 or 15.

2 With the database window displayed, select the **REPORTS** object type, highlight one of the reports you have created and click on the **DESIGN** button. The report will be displayed with its components clearly marked. These components and their roles are summarised in the table below. Note that Report Wizard creates reports with default settings in many areas.

3 Examine the report you have displayed. Click on each control in turn. Examine the default settings for the various components of a report.

Component	Description
Report header	Contains any headings or other introductory text that might appear at the beginning of the report
Page header	Contains headings that will appear at the top of each page, such as a running title and page numbers
Detail	Shows data from the records in the database. Sets up the format for records in general, which is then used for every

	record to be included in the report
Page footer	Appears at the bottom of the page
Report footer	Contains information at the end of the report, such as a final summary or a statement such as 'this is the end of the report'
Group header	Marks the beginning of a group, usually introduces the group the report will display
Group footer	Marks the end of a group and often contains sections that summarise the records that are part of a group

Creating a blank report

Create a blank report for the **Session** table, showing all the fields in the table, thus:

1. Select the **REPORTS** object type in the database window and then click the **NEW** button in the database window. Select the **Session** table from the **CHOOSE THE TABLE OR QUERY...** drop-down list box.

2. Select the **DESIGN VIEW** option.

3. Consider the layout and decide where to put the title, field labels and the fields themselves.

4. Add all the fields to the report from the field list. Display the field list. Double-click on the **FIELD LIST** title bar to highlight all the fields.

5. Click and drag the highlighted fields on to the detail section of the report. Controls for all the fields should appear.

6. Save as **Sessions** and close.

Extra windows

When you create a new blank report, the toolbox window will be displayed. This is useful for adding controls to the report. There are a number of such windows you will encounter as you advance in report design. These are as follows:

Window	Function
Properties sheet	to change different features of the report's contents
Field list	to add controls bound to fields
Toolbox	to select the design tool required (can be dragged to left of screen where it 'locks' as a toolbar)

All these windows can be moved or closed in the same way as any other window. They can also be opened and closed from the **VIEW** menu.

Changing an existing Report Wizard's report

To change the look of an existing report the positions of controls and their size can be altered.

In order to move a control, the control must first be selected and then it can be moved by dragging it. The different types of controls can be selected in the same way as controls are selected and moved on forms. If you need a reminder, see 'Moving and sizing controls' in Topic 12.

We wish to improve on the design of the report **Total Health and Fitness Clients** so the final report looks like Figure 17.1.

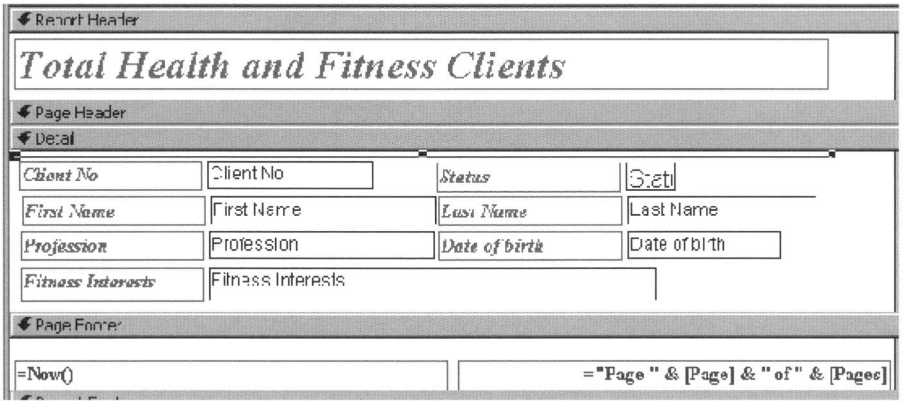

FIGURE 17.1

1. First, open the existing report. Select the report **Total Health and Fitness Clients** in the database window and then select the **DESIGN** button.

2. Now move the controls on the report until it resembles the design screen shown in Figure 17.1, using the instructions above for selecting and moving controls. If the toolbox is in the way, remove it by using **VIEW – TOOLBOX**.

   Note: If you get into a muddle in your first attempt to move controls, remember controls can be deleted. Select them and use the **DELETE** key. If all else fails close **without saving** and start again.

3. View the new report on screen using Print Preview.

4. Save the report as **Total Health and Fitness Clients2** using **FILE – SAVE AS**.

Further customisation of a report

We wish to open the report **Sessions** we created earlier and to modify the layout of the field labels as indicated below, in order to create a report like the one shown overleaf:

Total Health and Fitness   Instructor-led Fitness Sessions

Session   Day 1 = Monday through to 7 = Sunday

1   Aqua Aerobics

           Session Day: 1   Instructor: Joy
           Session Time: 10:00   Gender Mix   Female

2   Body Pump

           Session Day: 1   Instructor: Andy
           Session Time: 19:00   Gender Mix   Male

3   Group Exercise

           Session Day: 1   Instructor: Rob
           Session Time: 15:00   Gender Mix   Mixed

1 First, open the report called **Sessions** by selecting the **REPORTS** object type in the database window, and then selecting the **DESIGN** button.

2 Click on the fields and their labels and move them into a position resembling that illustrated above. Remove the labels for **Session No** and **Activity** and move these controls together at the top of the detail section.

3 To align a group of controls, you may wish to use **FORMAT – ALIGN – LEFT** (select them as a group first).

4 If you inadvertently delete a field, display the **FIELD LIST** window and drag the field on to the report.

5 Press **ENTER** or click on another part of the report to crystallise changes.

6 Experiment with aligning groups of controls in order to improve the report's appearance.

7 If a header and footer section are not visible, create them by choosing **VIEW – REPORT HEADER/FOOTER** so that a tick is placed beside this option.

Next, create a control box in the report header into which you can insert text, thus:

8 With the toolbox displayed, click on the **LABEL** tool. Place the pointer in the Report Header box and drag it to create a box large enough to accommodate text.

9 Key the following text in to the report header band: *Total Health and Fitness*; add further text *Instructor-led Fitness Sessions* and also some text indicating the days of the week numbering scheme. Add a *Sessions* label at the lower left part of the header section.

10 Add the date to the report footer by using **INSERT – DATE AND TIME**, selecting a suitable format, clicking on **OK** and dragging the control to the report footer section.

11 Print Preview the report, save the report Sessions and close it.

Changing the report and section areas

To alter the depth of a section of the form:

Move the pointer to the bottom edge of the section where it will change shape. Drag the pointer to a new location.

To alter the area of the report:

Drag the right and bottom edges to the size you require.

Further reformatting of a report

This task reformats the report created in the last task to create a report with a different format and saved as Sessions2. You will create the report illustrated below:

Total Health and Fitness

Instructor-led Fitness Sessions   Day1 = Monday through to 7 = Sunday

Session No	Day	Time	Instructor	Activity	Gender Mix
1	1	10:00	Joy	Aqua Aerobics	Female
2	1	19:00	Andy	Body Pump	Male
3	1	15:00	Rob	Group Exercise	Mixed
4	1	19:00	Diane	Low Impact Aerobics	Mixed
5	2	10:00	Andy	Sport performance	Male
6	2	14:00	Diane	High Impact Aerobics	Female

Changes made are to format the text of labels; to add text and controls to the page header and footer sections; to select and format headings as a group; and to use text alignment in text boxes.

1 Open the report called Sessions in DESIGN mode.

2 Select the controls in the REPORT HEADER and make them larger and apply a different font. Click on the CENTER alignment button to centre the text within the control. If necessary resize the control box to display all the text.

3 Remove the Gender Mix control by selecting it, pressing the DELETE key. Display the page header and footer sections using VIEW – PAGE HEADER/ FOOTER.

4 Move the field labels into the page header band by first selecting them as a group. Choose EDIT – CUT and click anywhere in the page header. Then

choose **EDIT – PASTE**.

5 Rearrange the labels in the page header so they are column headings. Select these labels as a group and format them by making them a different font.

6 Adjust the size of the page header so it accommodates the labels by dragging the bottom of the page header.

7 Using **INSERT – PAGE NUMBERS** and **INSERT DATE AND TIME** insert these controls into the page footer.

8 In the detail section, rearrange the controls to align them under the respective labels in the page header. If necessary, expand the boxes to accommodate the longest field value. For example, make sure the control box for **Activity** accommodates **High Impact Aerobics**.

9 In turn, select the text boxes for **Session No** and **Time** and left justify them by clicking on the **ALIGN LEFT** button.

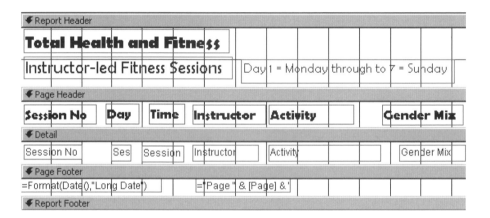

10 Print Preview, save as **Sessions2**, close and print as required.

Note: It will probably be necessary to move back and forth between Print Preview and Design mode a few times as you make changes and would like to view the results of those changes.

Tools in the report design window

The report design window has a number of tools you have been benefitting from in designing a report. It is useful briefly to review these:

- The **RULER** measures the distance from the top and left corner of the report. The ruler can be removed or replaced by choosing **VIEW – RULER**.
- The **GRID** appears in Design view. Access automatically aligns moved or sized controls with the grid. The grid can be moved or replaced by choosing **VIEW – GRID**. To deactivate the grid choose **FORMAT – SNAP TO GRID**.
- The **ALIGN** option. Use **FORMAT – ALIGN** to position controls relative to each other. Select controls, choose **FORMAT – ALIGN** and the appropriate alignment (e.g. Left).

Customising a groups/totals report

1 Create a report that groups all the sessions offered by the centre, based on the **Session** table, according to **Activity**.

2 Using the Report Wizard, base the report on the **Session** table, and add all the fields except **Session No**.

3 Group the report by **Activity** and sort the report in **Instructor** order. Choose a stepped layout, portrait, bold style report format.

4 Save this report as **Session List**. View the report in Design view. Select the **Instructor** control and display the **PROPERTIES** window. Set the **HIDE DUPLICATES** property to **YES**.

5 Preview the report. You could also do this for **Gender Mix**. Hiding duplicates can make a report look less cluttered. Save the report.

91

TOPIC 18

Adding controls to forms

Topic objectives

A typical windows includes a wide variety of different controls, such as option buttons, check boxes and list boxes.

This topic will show you how to add the following controls to forms:

- a calculated text box
- a list box
- an option group
- a combo box
- a check box.

Types of form controls

In creating forms and reports in the earlier topics, you have met labels and text box controls. Windows applications use a wide range of other types of control, such as list boxes, option buttons and option groups. If the entry for a control can be selected from a list (for example, client status), data entry can be made more efficient by allowing this selection to be performed by clicking on one entry in a list box. List boxes reduce error and maintain consistency and are faster to use.

There are three categories of control:

1. *Bound* controls. A bound control is associated with (bound to) a field in the table or query that was used to create the form. Text boxes are the most common form of bound control. Data can be displayed or entered using a bound control.

2. *Unbound* controls. An unbound control is independent of the data in the form's table or query. Labels used as titles are examples of unbound controls.

3. *Calculated* controls. A calculated control is an expression. Usually the expression performs a calculation upon data in the form's table or query.

The toolbox

The Access toolbox offers a selection of tools by which controls and text may be added to forms: the Field List shows a list of fields in the table or query the form was based upon; and the Properties sheet is a list of properties. The list of properties will depend upon what part of the form is selected.

The toolbox only appears when you are in Design mode. To display the

toolbox, click on the **TOOLBOX** button or use **VIEW** – **TOOLBOX**. To display the field list click on the **FIELD LIST** button or choose **VIEW** – **FIELD LIST**. To display the **PROPERTIES** sheet click on the **PROPERTIES** button on the toolbar or choose **VIEW** – **PROPERTIES**.

Colour selection can be made using the drop-down buttons on the formatting toolbar. These will be considered in Topic 20.

Creating a calculated text box

When people join Total Health and Fitness, they pay a subscription for the following year that runs from the date on which they joined. They renew their membership annually. To calculate whether the client's subscription is overdue, the renewal date is compared with today's date. If the renewal date is before today's date, the fee is overdue. To create a realistic number of clients who are late renewing their membership, say three, amend or add records to the **Client** table with appropriate dates for renewal.

In this task the calculated control that is to be created is one that identifies clients whose renewal is due. This control will be added to the **Client** form created in Topics 11 and 12.

1 Open the **Client** table using the **OPEN** button to display the data.

93

2 View each record in turn and look at the **Date of Last Renewal** field.

3 Make amendments, if necessary, to the **Date of Last Renewal** fields so some clients have a date of renewal before exactly one year ago from today and others after that date.

To add the calculated text box:

4 Open the **Client** form in Design view.

5 Click on the text box tool in the toolbox.

6 Click on a suitable place on the form for the text box and its label.

7 Edit the label to read *Status Fee* :

8 Click in the text box and key in the expression:

=iif(DateAdd("d",365,[Date of last renewal])<Date(),"Overdue","Up to date")

If you miss out a bracket, when you press **ENTER**, Access will display an information box. Click on **OK** and you will be returned to the control so you can edit the expression. If you have trouble seeing this expression you can display it in a zoom box by selecting **CONTROL SOURCE** in the **PROPERTIES** sheet and pressing **SHIFT+F2** to open the zoom box for editing.

Name	Status Fee
Control Source	=IIf(DateAdd("d",365,[Date of last renewal])<Date(),"Overdue","Up to date")

9 Edit the name in the text box property window to read **Status Fee**.

10 Run the form. If you have errors return to the Design view and check you have keyed in the expression correctly. For example, if you have misspelt the control name, then the message **#NAME?** appears in the control. Check all control names carefully and correct them.

Note: If you rename a control in an underlying table but do not update the field labels on the form, this kind of error will occur. Sort out the field names to match each other in the expression, table and form.

11 Save the form.

Note: The expression you have just used above is an in-line IF...THEN...ELSE statement. DateAdd adds one year to the date of the last renewal. This is compare to today's date. IF the result is less than today's date THEN the subscription is overdue ELSE it is up to date.

If you wish to create your own expressions, refer to the Access Office Assistant for lists of functions available.

Adding a list box

List boxes are useful for picking values from a list of options. You may define a list or use a table as a source of the list. The example that will be considered is that of adding a list box to the **Session** form. The list box will be defined for the **Gender Mix** field and will use a static list.

1 To add a list box to the **Session** form, first open the form in Design mode.

2 Select and delete the **Gender Mix** text box.

3 Open the **FIELD LIST** window and choose **Gender Mix**.

4 Check that the Control Wizard button in the toolbox is depressed and click on the **LIST BOX** tool.

5 Adjust the controls on the form so there is room to have a list box approximately deep enough to show all three choices in the form. If the list box is made smaller it will be shown with a vertical scroll bar.

7 Click on the **LIST BOX** tool in the toolbox.

8 Click and drag the **Gender Mix** field from the field list window to the former position of the **Gender Mix** text box.

9 The List Box Wizard dialog box displays (provided the Control Wizard button in the toolbox is depressed). Select the option **I WILL TYPE IN THE VALUES THAT I WANT** and click on **NEXT>**.

9 Enter *1* into the **NUMBER OF COLUMNS** box. Click in the first cell and key in *Fitness Suite*. Complete the column with *Male*, *Female*, and *Mixed* so that there are three rows in column 1. Click on **NEXT>**.

10 Choose the option **STORE THAT VALUE IN THIS FIELD** and click on **NEXT>**.

11 Entitle the label for the list box **_Gender Mix_** (see Figure 18.1) and click on
FINISH.

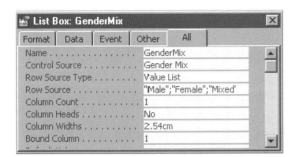

FIGURE 18.1

12 Click on the form **VIEW** button on the toolbar to display the form. If
adjustments to the position of controls are needed, return to the Design mode
to make them. The form could look something like Figure 18.2.

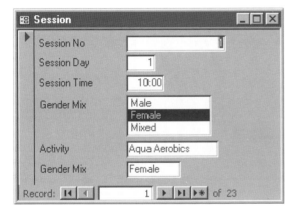

FIGURE 18.2

95

13 Save the form as **Session2**. Try using the form to enter another session. Close
the form.

Adding option groups

Option buttons are commonly employed in Windows applications to select one option
from a set of choices. An option group will be added to the **Client** form.

1 Open the form in Design mode.

2 Adjust the area of the form to allow room for the option group at the bottom or
side of the form.

3 Click on the **OPTION GROUP FRAME** tool in the toolbox.
Check that the Control Wizard button in toolbox is depressed.

4 Choose **Status** from the **FIELD LIST** and **DRAG TO** the form.
Dragging is important as it links the control with the field.
Release at a suitable position.

5 Enter the label names and click on **NEXT>**.

6 Select the option **NO, I DON'T WANT A DEFAULT** and click on **NEXT>**.

7 The default values are correct, so click on **NEXT>**.

8 Choose the option **STORE THE VALUE IN THIS FIELD: STATUS** and click on **NEXT>**.

9 Choose the option buttons type of control with an etched style and click on **NEXT>**.

10 Give the option group the title *Status* and click on **FINISH**.

11 To test the form, click on the **FORM VIEW** button. The already-existing **Status** text box control should serve to confirm the entry in the option group. Data could be entered into this field using either of the controls. Experiment by entering a new **Client's** record.

12 Save the form as **Client**.

13 Open the **Session2** form and, in a similar way, replace the **Session Day** control with an option group as illustrated in Figure 18.3. Save and close the form.

FIGURE 18.3

96

Adding a combo box

In this task, a combo box will be added to the **Session2** form for the choice of instructor. The current instructors will be listed but the text box will accept an alternative that may be keyed in.

1 Open the **Session2** form in Design view.

2 Select and delete the **Instructor** text box.

3 Check that both the field list window and the toolbox are displayed. Check the Control Wizard button in the toolbox is depressed.

4 Click on the **COMBO BOX** tool in the toolbox. Click and drag the **Instructor** field from the field list on to its former location on the form.

5 Using the Wizard, opt to key in the values and set the number of columns to 1.

6 Enter the list of regular instructors, *Joy*, *Andy*, *Rob* and *Barry*.

7 Choose the store in instructor field option and edit the label if required. Click on **FINISH**.

8 Click on the **FORM VIEW** button on the toolbar to display the form. The **Instructor** text box should have a list box button, which, when clicked, will display the list of instructors. If adjustments are needed, return to Design mode. When complete, save the form. Experiment with entering data in order to see how the combo box works.

Instructor	Joy ▼
	Joy
	Andy
	Rob
	Barry

Adding controls to reports

Topic objectives

Controls can be used in reports to show calculations or to summarise group reports.

This topic will show you how to:

- save a form as a report
- add a calculated control to a report
- create groups within a report.

Saving a form as a report

If you change a form to a report, you have more control over the variety of ways in which the data can be formatted for printing. For example, you can create a group/totals report from the data.

In this task the **Reservation** form will be saved as a report:

1. In the database window with the **FORMS** object type selected click on the form **Reservation** using the right mouse button.

2. Choose **SAVE AS** from the shortcut menu. In the **SAVE FORM 'RESERVATION' TO:** box, edit the text to read *Reservation*, open the **AS** drop-down list box, select **REPORT** and click on **OK**.

3. Select the **REPORTS** object type in the database window.

4. Select the **Reservation** report and preview it.

5. Use **SORTING AND GROUPING** to group the report in location order and to sort in date and time order.

6. Adjust the design as necessary before printing.

Adding a calculated control to a report

Calculated controls are useful in reports. If a report has been produced from a table that contains data about stock in the form of quantity sold and price, the sales revenue can be calculated by multiplying the quantity sold by the price.

A calculated control was used in the **Client** form to find out whether a client's annual fee was overdue or not. In this task, this control will be copied and pasted into the report **Total Health and Fitness Clients2** customised in Topic 17.

1. Open the **Client** form in Design view. Select the calculated control and copy it, using **EDIT – COPY**. Close the form.

2 Open the report **Total Health and Fitness Clients2** in Design mode.

3 Click on the detail bar and use **EDIT – PASTE** to paste in the control. Move it to a suitable place and, if necessary, rearrange the other controls.

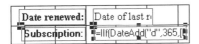

4 Save the report, preview and print it. The new control should print either the text 'Up to date' or 'Overdue'.

Using a nested IIf control

Session days are entered as a number, and it would be useful to read the day of the week in a report. One way to do this is to use an option group in exactly the same way as for a form (previous topic). Another way is to use a nested IIf.

1 Display the **Sessions2** report in design mode. Click on the Text box tool in the toolbox and click on the report near to the **Session Day** control. You may need to adjust the positions of the controls.

2 In the text box enter the following expression, taking care to get the brackets correct.

=IIf([Session Day]=1,"Monday",IIf([Session Day]=2,"Tuesday",IIf([Session Day]=3,"Wednesday",IIf([Session Day]=4,"Thursday",IIf([Session Day]=5,"Friday",IIf([Session Day]=6,"Saturday","Sunday"))))))

3 Remove the label for this text box and adjust its size so that, when the report is previewed, 'Wednesday' will fit into the control. Preview the report, save and print if required. Note that, having created this control, it can be simply copied and pasted into other reports and forms where appropriate.

Adding calculated controls to a grouped report

1 Display the **Total Health and Fitness Clients2** report in Design mode.

2 Click on the **SORTING AND GROUPING** button on the toolbar and set the sorting and grouping as in Figure 19.1. This report sorts the clients into alphabetical order within the Status groups. For **Status**, set the **GROUP HEADER** and **GROUP FOOTER** to **YES**, and set **KEEP TOGETHER** to **WITH FIRST DETAIL**, which will prevent a page break between the group heading and a following detail.

3 Move the control for the **Status** to the **Status** group header. Select the control use **EDIT – CUT**. Click on the status header bar and use **EDIT – PASTE**.

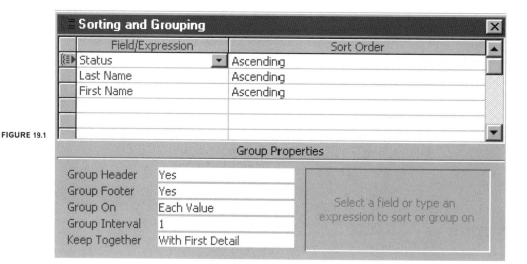

FIGURE 19.1

④ In the **Status** group footer, add a text box control and key into it the expression **=Count([Client No[)** which will display the total number of clients in each category.

⑤ Add a label that says ***Number of Clients***

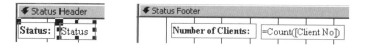

⑥ Preview the report, save and print it.

Groups within groups in a report

Continue with the **Total Health and Fitness Clients2** report. The aim is to adjust this report so that groups by town are created within each client status group.

① Display the report in Design view and display the sorting and grouping dialog box. In the fourth row, add the field **Town**. Select this row and drag it to below the first row. Priority of grouping can be changed by rearranging the rows in the **SORTING AND GROUPING** dialog box.

② Select **YES** for group header and group footer.

③ In Report Design mode, move the control for **Town** to the **TOWN GROUP HEADER**.

④ Copy the calculated control for number of clients from the **STATUS GROUP FOOTER** and paste the copy into the **TOWN GROUP FOOTER**. Amend the labels for both these controls so you know which is which.

⑤ Preview the report, save and print it.

⑥ Experiment with different sortings and groupings.

Concatenating controls in a report

Sometimes the printouts in reports can look rather bitty because they have too much space between them. An example of this is people's names. One way to reduce the extra space is to use the **TRIM** function and to 'add' controls together.

1 Open the **Total Health and Fitness Clients2** report in Design view. Remove the controls for **First Name and Last Name**.

2 Add a text box and edit its label to read **Name:** and its text box to read:

=Trim([Title])+" "+Trim([First Name])+" "+Trim([Last Name])

3 Set the border for this control as for the others and preview the report.

Text and controls can be used together to give much neater printouts. For example, in a status group footer the following could be used:

="Total number of clients "+count([Client No])+ " in status "+[Status]

Forms and reports: graphical design

Topic objectives

This topic investigates features that allow you to adjust the appearance of the information on a report or form, and to make their presentation more exciting. Access offers a wide range of tools for the imaginative formatting of both screens and reports. Whilst all these features can be applied to both forms and reports, some features are used more often with forms and others are used more often with reports.

You can make a control look three-dimensional, add colour or set borders to different widths to make reports and forms look more exciting. Remember that, since most reports are not printed in colour, colours are most likely to be useful for on-screen forms and do not normally need to be set for reports. Equally, three-dimensional controls are particularly useful on forms, where they may be used to highlight labels or to mark out a button.

This topic will show you how to:

- add lines and boxes to forms and reports
- use different alignments and fonts
- apply setting, colours, borders and three-dimensional effects.

Understanding design

Access provides a number of tools with which you can improve the look of forms and reports that you design. You will already have used some of these briefly in the last few topics. Forms and reports created using Wizards use some design features to a limited extent, but by the time you have completed this topic you should be able to improve on Wizard designs.

Although the tools we explore here allow you to be very adventurous with your designs, remember good design hinges on the appropriate and sparing use of objects such as boxes and lines, and upon the use of only a limited number of different fonts and colours. In addition, most organisations will wish to establish a house style that might be applied to all screen forms and groups of similar reports. We are not this consistent in the forms and reports we generate in these topics, because the range of forms and reports used here has been used to demonstrate the wide range of features and designs that can be adopted. When, however, you do need to create a house style, form and report templates are one means of doing this. We introduce these briefly in the next topic. The tips below act as a reminder of good design features.

Design tips: forms

- Keep the form simple and easy to read. Don't use unnecessary text and graphics, but do use fonts and font sizes that are easy to read on the screen.
- Use colour sparingly to make forms interesting, but choose colours that are

comfortable for those working at the screen for a long period of time.

☐ Design the form taking into account how it will be used (i.e. layout of text boxes and ease of movement between them (TabOrder)).

☐ Maintain a consistent appearance for related forms. This looks more professional and makes it easier for a user to acclimatise to a series of forms.

Design tips: reports

☐ Keep the report simple. Make the data easy to read by choosing font sizes and types that print well. Use fonts and graphics to help to convey important messages in the report.

☐ Design in the knowledge of the capabilities of the printer. In particular, colour printers can produce much more intricate detail than non-colour printers.

☐ Consider how the report is going to be used. Who are the readers, and why will they be using the report?

Adding lines and rectangles to forms and reports

Lines and rectangles can be added to reports and forms to emphasise portions of the form or report, or to separate one part of the form or report form another.

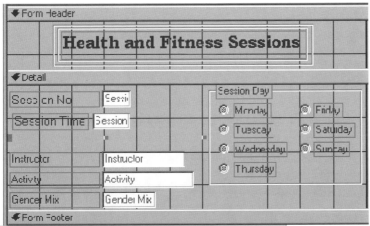

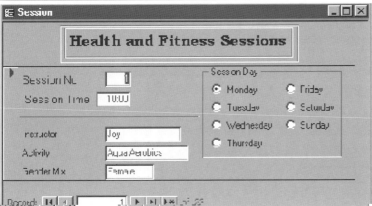

FIGURE 20.1

1. Open the form **Session2.** Move and size the controls so they are in the position shown in Figure 20.1. Select the **LINE** tool in the toolbox.

2. Point to where you want the line to start. Drag the pointer. The **LINE** tool draws a line from where you start dragging the pointer to where you release the mouse. Create a line as shown in the figure.

3. Add a header to the form as illustrated. Select the **RECTANGLE** tool in the toolbox.

4. Point to where you want the rectangle to start. Drag the pointer to where you want the opposite corner to be so you create a rectangle around the text.

5. Draw another rectangle around the text in the form header.

6. Select one of the rectangles by clicking on it and practise deleting it by pressing the **DELETE** key. You are likely to need to delete lines or rectangles you have placed in the wrong place before you have finished!

7. Recreate the rectangle. Note that if you later choose a fill for either or both of these rectangles, you will need to use **FORMAT – SEND TO BACK** to send the filled rectangle behind the existing controls on the form.

8. Insert a line underneath the **Session Time** control. Try repositioning the option group controls to produce two columns in the list.

9. Save the form **Session2.**

Changing control layers

When you add rectangles (or other objects) to a form or report, they are initially placed on top of any other controls. The default fill of rectangles is transparent, so any controls already on the form or report that are bounded by the rectangle will still be visible.

If you set a fill for the rectangle (see later), it will cover existing controls. In order to display controls that have been covered, you need to send the covering object behind the existing controls.

Select the covering object or control and choose **FORMAT – SEND TO BACK** to send it behind controls and objects it has hidden. To bring a control from behind other controls and to put it on top, choose **FORMAT – BRING TO FRONT**.

Setting alignment and font

To set alignment or font, first select the control to which you wish to add style and then click on an appropriate icon on the toolbar as required:

Alignment

≡ left alignment ≡ centres text ≡ right alignment

Font

 Font name which sets the style of characters

Font size which sets the size of the characters

 Bold, which sets characters as bold

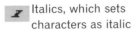 Italics, which sets characters as italic

 Underline, which sets characters as underline

Setting alignment and fonts on forms

1 Open the form **Session2.**

2 Increase the font size of the **Session No**, **Day** and **Time** labels. You may also need to increase the size of the controls in order to accommodate the text of the labels and the data in the larger size.

3 Click on each control in turn and check its alignment. Left align controls for all fields except **Session No, Day** and **Time**, which should be right aligned. Save and close the form.

Borders, lines, alignment and fonts on reports

1 Design a new report **Sessions3** based on the **Session** table in a similar way to the **Sessions2** report created in Topic 17.

2 In the report header, insert two controls and key in the text shown in the following figures. Move the controls to centre them. Centre align the text in the controls. Format the text to an appropriately large size and bold. Insert a box around the text. Use **FORMAT – SEND TO BACK** to put the box behind the controls.

3 In the detail band, first add the controls using the field list. Click on the **FIELD LIST** window title bar to select all fields, and then drag one of the fields to where you want the fields to start within the detail band. Fields and their field names will be added to the detail band.

4 Edit the field names so they match those shown in Figure 20.2. Move the controls to match the arrangement in the illustration.

5 Format the text in the controls to a slightly larger size and size the controls appropriately.

6 To align a group of controls, select the group and apply **FORMAT – ALIGN – LEFT/RIGHT**. Most of these controls are left aligned with respect to each other.

7 Next, examine the alignment of text within the controls. Ensure all controls are left aligned and, in particular, remember to left align **Time**.

8 Insert a box around the **Session No** control and label. Insert a further box to enclose all text in the detail band and send it to the back or set its fill property to transparent.

Design view

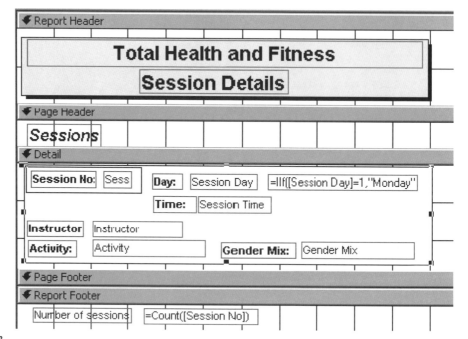

FIGURE 20.2

Print Preview

9 Key the text **Sessions** in the page header band and apply appropriate formatting.

10 At the top of the page footer band insert a line. Add an unbound control using the count function to total the number of sessions.

11 Examine the report in Print Preview, noting especially you have made your controls large enough to display their information.

12 Make any necessary adjustments, Print Preview again, and save the report Sessions3.

Alignment and font

Text alignment determines whether the characters that appear in a text box or label start at the left edge of the box or label, end at the right edge or are centred with the control. The default alignment is right alignment for data fields containing numbers and dates, and left alignment for all other controls.

Whilst designing your form or report it is useful to examine the alignment of text box and label controls. To do this, select the control by clicking on it, and then examine which of the alignment buttons is depressed. The best alignment depends on how the controls have been arranged on the form or report. For example, in a report showing data in columns with field labels in the page header, set the alignment of the headers to the same as that for the entries below them in order to align the headings with the data.

A *font* is a collection of features that describes how the text appears. Using two or three different fonts, and using a larger font size or bold or italics, can emphasise parts of a report and make your form or report more interesting.

Note: Although it is possible to set every control to a different font, good design requires you be selective in the use of a range of fonts. In particular, you might consider the following:

- Do not use more than two or three fonts on one report or form.
- Select a font that is appropriate for the application. For example, script and other fancy fonts are not often used in business applications and, where they are used, they are used deliberately for effect.

Special effects, colours and borders

The formatting toolbar (available in Form and Report design) allows the colour, border and special effects of controls, labels and objects to be set.

Each drop-down button allows the control of fill/back color, font/fore color, line/border color, line/border width and special effects.

An alternative way to set these properties is through the **PROPERTY SHEET** window. This can be displayed by double-clicking on the control or area whose properties are to be viewed and changed. Generally, it is easier to use the formatting toolbar, so we shall restrict ourselves to its use here.

107

Setting dimensions and borders

Open the form **Session2** and use the form to experiment with setting dimensions, colours and borders. For example, try:

- setting all the field labels as raised
- setting the form header as sunken
- selecting the line in the detail band and making it wider
- applying some colours to different parts of the screen to make it look interesting.

Back, fore and border colours

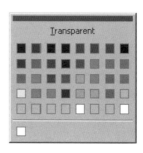

A control can have separate colours for back (ground) fore (ground) and border. To set a colour, select the control (or colours) and click on the drop-down arrow of the fill/back color, font/fore color and line/border color buttons to drop down the colour selection box, and choose an appropriate colour. If the **TRANSPARENT** button in the colour selection box is clicked, the selected control becomes transparent so the control shows whatever controls are behind it.

Try out different colour combinations until you have chosen one that is legible and draws attention to appropriate parts of the screen. Remember to use colour sparingly and sensibly.

Border widths

Border controls can be set at different widths. Some controls, such as the labels for check boxes, option buttons and text boxes, have as a default zero width (no border). Other controls, such as option groups, list boxes, and combo boxes, have as default a thin black border.

To select a border width, click on the drop-down arrow of the **BORDER WIDTH** button on the toolbar. From the selection shown, choose an appropriate border width.

Special effects

Special effects give a 3-D look to your design. They can be set as one of the following types: flat, raised, sunken, etched, shadowed, and chiselled. These options are displayed by clicking on the drop-down arrow of the **SPECIAL EFFECTS** button on the toolbar.

Notes:

- When you select a special effect, the control adopts the same colours as buttons on the toolbar and command buttons to achieve the effect. These colours are set by the Control Panel display settings. It is only possible to change the fore and back colours.
- If a special effect such as raised, sunken, etched, shadowed or chiselled is chosen for control, changing the border width will cause the control to revert to flat and the default colour.

TOPIC 21

Forms and reports: control properties and templates

Topic objectives

When a form or report is created without using a Wizard, Access uses a template to define the default characteristics of the form or report. Controls have predetermined properties which we have modified to improve the look of the form or report. It is possible to change the default properties of controls, which then apply to all the controls of that type when added to a form or report.

However, any modified default properties you set will belong to the particular form or report only. If you want to use a set of default control properties for multiple forms or reports, you can create templates that store default settings and then use these templates whenever you create forms and reports.

A template for producing reports or forms can be used in order to maintain a house style in form or report design or, more simply, to avoid having to format all sections of the form or report on each occasion.

This topic will show you how to:

- examine the default properties of a control
- set default properties of a control.
- create a form and report template.

While it is useful to note that it is possible to modify the default settings for a number of different types of controls, we do not recommend you attempt this until you are sure you understand which settings you are changing. There is immense potential for getting into an irretrievable muddle once you start to modify default settings. Proceed with caution!

Examining the default properties of a control

To minimise the danger of you modifying the default settings in ways in which you did not intend and thereby finding it difficult to follow later activities in this book, this task concentrates on examining the existing default settings rather than modifying them. **Note that adjustments to default settings will apply thereafter to the chosen form or report until they are again changed**.

To set property defaults for a form or report you follow steps similar to those for property setting.

1 Open any form or report.

2 Select a section control by clicking on it. Click on the label button in the **TOOLBOX**. Open the **PROPERTY SHEET** window. The **PROPERTY SHEET**

window changes to show only the properties you can set as the default for controls of the selected type (e.g. text, date or number).

③ The title bar changes to 'Default' and the name of the object. Most of the properties listed you should recognise from earlier activities when you were setting the properties of the individual controls. Examine the default properties for this tool.

④ In a similar way, examine the **PROPERTY SHEET** window for a text box control.

⑤ Again, similarly, examine the **PROPERTY SHEET** window for a box or a line.

⑥ The properties in the **PROPERTY SHEET** window can be changed just as you would change the properties for selected controls or parts of forms or reports. Figure 21.1 shows the Default Properties box for a header section in a form, showing the Special Effect property drop-down list box.

FIGURE 21.1

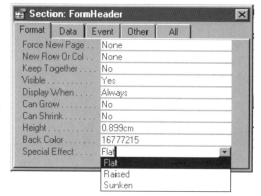

⑦ Any control of that type you subsequently add to the form or report uses the new settings you have made for the control.

What are some of the differences between the defaults that are set for these different types of controls?

Text box properties

As a text box is the most common control, it is worth while dwelling on some of the default properties you might wish to change for your own database applications. These are as follows:

Property	Description
Auto Label	Causes labels to appear with, for example, text boxes
Add Colon	Causes colons to appear at the end of labels
Label X and Label Y	Set the relative distance from the upper left-hand corner of the selected control
Label Align	Sets the position of the text in the label

Creating a form/report template from an existing form/report

Create a form or report on which the settings for the controls are as you want them to be. Display the form or report header and footer and page header and footer, if you also want these to be included in the default. Set section sizes to determine their default size, if you want these included. Save this form or report.

To use the form or report as a template, choose **TOOLS – OPTIONS** and click on the **FORMS/REPORTS** tab. Key in a name for the form/report template in the Form Template or Report Template box. Click on **OK**. When you next create a new blank report, the selected report or form will be used as a template.

Note: The default form template and report template are **NORMAL**.

Creating and using a report template based on an existing report

An existing report can be used to define the properties of a template. The most obvious properties that will be set are the section sizes (e.g. the size of the page header) and the presence or absence of various headers and footers. Other section and control properties have also been set.

1. Open the report **Sessions3** in Design view.

2. Make any modifications to the design you would like in the template (for example, adjusting the size of the report header and footer, and page header and footer). Save the report.

3. Next, to set the report as a template, choose **TOOLS – OPTIONS** and click on the **FORMS/REPORTS** tab.

4. In the Report Template box at the bottom of the dialog box, enter the name of the report **Sessions3**.

5. Click on **OK**, and this will be used as the default report template.

6. Now, create a new blank report (*note*: report may be based on a table or query) without using the Wizard.

7. You should see that this report has the same headers and footers and section sizes as the template. Close the report without saving.

Setting up, creating and using a form template

If an existing form or report is not available, a blank form or report can be opened and properties defined to be stored in the template.

1. First, create a form template by selecting the forms type and choosing **NEW** and clicking on Design view without basing the form on a table or query.

2. Display the form header and footer to include these in the template. Adjust the size of these if desired. Set the label default properties to Times New Roman, size 14.

3. Set background and foreground colours. Save this form as **THF form template**.

4. Set this form as a template, choosing **TOOLS – OPTIONS** and click on the **FORMS/REPORTS** tab.

5. In the **FORM TEMPLATE** box, enter the name of the form **THF form template**.

6. Click on **OK**, and this will be used as the form template.

7. Now, create a blank new form (*note*: form may be based on a table or query) without using the Wizard.

8. The form has the same headers and footers and section sizes as the template. Test the label tool and you should see it has the properties as set in the template. Close this form without saving.

Returning form and report templates to normal

To return the form and report templates to normal:

1. Choose **TOOLS – OPTIONS** and click on the **FORMS/REPORTS** tab.

2. In the **FORM TEMPLATE** text box, enter **NORMAL** and repeat for **REPORT TEMPLATE**.

3. Click on **OK**.

Relationships between tables

Topic objectives

All the exercises in this book up to this point use tables one at a time. You have created and used a number of tables, but these are all separate. The real power of a database application comes from being able to link tables together and to use data from more than one table, in say, reports.

This topic will show you how to:

- define and create relationships between tables
- apply referential integrity.

Defining relationships between tables

The relationships between the tables in the **Total Health and Fitness** database application (as we want to define them) are shown in Figure 22.2 (see later in this topic). Figure 22.2 shows all the tables you have created to date, with the links we wish to make between those table. First however, it might be useful to pause and think about the purpose of these links. An example may assist here.

To discover the annual fee a client has paid, and to display it alongside the client's name, it is necessary to locate one item of data in the **Client** table and another in the **Client Status** table. We can link the records through the **Status No** field which will appear in both tables. Accordingly, in Access we need to define a link between these two tables through **Status No**, as illustrated in Figure 22.1.

In the above example, we could, of course, have kept the annual fee in the **Client** table in our database. If, for example, there was no **Client Status** table, and the data was stored in the **Client** table, the fee needs to be stored with each client. This means storing the fee a large number of times instead of the limited number of times it is recorded in the **Client Status** table. Accordingly, using two tables instead of one saves space. Another advantage is the fees can be amended and the new data is then available throughout the database simultaneously, without updating numerous individual client records.

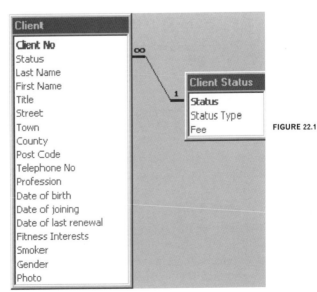

FIGURE 22.1

There are three kinds of relationships:

- *one-to-one* relationships
- *one-to-many* relationships
- *many-to-many* relationships.

A one-to-one relationship between two tables means that, for a particular field in one table there is one matching record only in the other table and vice versa. Commonly, this is a link between primary keys in both tables. An example could be the creation of a table to hold fitness details of clients undertaking a personal fitness programme. In this table there would be one record per client and **Client No** would be the primary key. The one-to-one link would be through **Client No** in both tables:

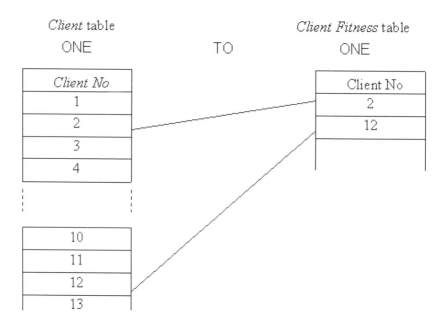

A one-to-many relationship means that, for one field in one table, there are lots of matching records in the other table. Commonly, this is a link between a primary key in the 'one' table and a matching field (often called a foreign key) in the 'many' table.

A many-to-many relationship means that, for one field in one table, there are lots of matching records in the other table and vice versa. This kind of relationship cannot be created directly in Access and database designers will introduce an extra table to break the relationship into two one-to-many relationships. For example, many **Customers** of a video hire outlet may borrow many **Videos.** By introducing a **Videos on Loan** table, this creates two one-to-many relationships out of the initial many-to-many one.

The commonest type of relationship is that of one-to-many, and it is the only type used in our system. Consider the relationship between a client and that client's reservations. A client may make no reservations, one reservation or several reservations. So one client can make several (many) reservations, a one-to-many relationship (i.e. there is only one record with that person's **Client No** in the **Client**

Client table
ONE

TO

Reservation table
MANY

Client No
1
2
3
4
5

Client No
8
2
6
8
2
18
5

table, yet there can be several records with that person's **Client No** in the **Reservation** table. **Client No** is the primary key in the **Client** table and **Client No** is a foreign key the **Reservation** table.

These relationships do not yet exist because they have not been defined. This topic concentrates on setting up these relationships. Note that relationships can be set up before any actual data is entered into any of the tables (common practice for professional database designers). Before any relationships between tables can be defined, the tables must be closed. It is important that, when a link is make between a field in one table and a field in another table, the two fields have the same data type, and it is good practice for them to have the same name.

115

Referential integrity

In the Edit Relationship dialog box (which appears when a relationship between tables is being created) there is an Enforce Referential Integrity check box. Consider the relationship between the **Client** and the **Reservation** table, we may want to stop a client number being entered into the **Reservation** table that does not exist in the **Client** table. By enforcing referential integrity, Access will check the **Client No** entered into the **Reservation** table against all the values held in **Client No** in the **Client** table and will prevent non-existent **Client No**s being entered.

Linking tables together

① Check you have created all the tables that are to be linked together in the database application. Make sure they are all closed (i.e. just the **DATABASE WINDOW** is left open).

2 Now the relationship between **Client No** in the **Client** table and **Client No** in the **Reservation** table can be created. The data type of the **Client No (Reservation)** is a long integer number, which is compatible with the data type AutoNumber of **Client No (Client)**. In one-to-many relationships the primary table in the relationship is the 'one' table, in this case the **Client** table, and the related table is the 'many' table (i.e. the **Reservation** table – a client can place many reservations). To define a relationship between tables:

3 Choose **TOOLS – RELATIONSHIPS** and the **RELATIONSHIPS** dialog box appears with the **SHOW TABLE** dialog box within it. If the **SHOW TABLE** dialog box does not appear, click on the **SHOW TABLE** button on the toolbar.

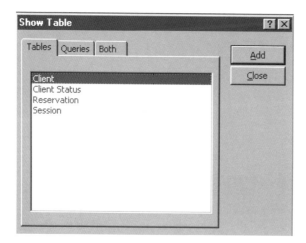

4 Select **Client** and click on **ADD**. Select **Reservation** and click on **ADD**. Click on **CLOSE.** The two table windows should be displayed and you may resize them if you wish.

5 To create the relationship, click on the **Client No** field in the **Client** table and drag to the **Client No** field in the **Reservation** table. Release and the **EDIT RELATIONSHIPS** dialog box is displayed.

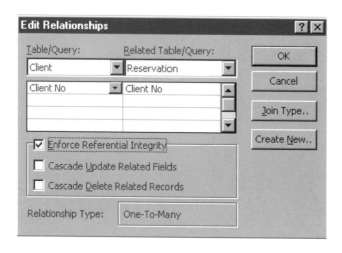

6 Click in the **ENFORCE REFERENTIAL INTEGRITY** check box and click on **OK**. The relationship between the tables will be shown.

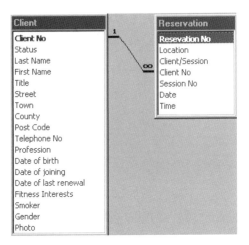

7 Use **FILE – SAVE** to save changes to the layout and close the **RELATIONSHIPS** window.

8 Using the same approach, create the other relationships indicated in Figure 22.2.

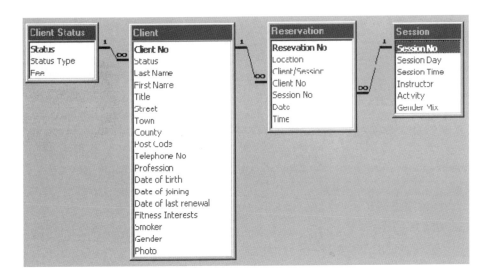

Queries using several tables

Topic objectives

In this topic queries that use more than one table are introduced. Tables are linked by their relationships and, through these links, can act as if they are one large table.

This topic will show you how to:

▢ create queries using multiple tables
▢ add and delete tables to or from a query.

In the last topic you have set up relationships between tables. In the interests of simplicity, queries previously created have been based on one table. In this topic we shall see that queries can use more than one table and that these queries can be used to produce forms or reports.

The versatility of a relational database comes from the way the tables are linked together. Queries using several tables are able to tap into the wealth of data effectively. If a client's address changes then only one change to the Client table is needed which would reflect in any query using that table.

Creating a query using several tables

When you use more than one table in a query, there should be links between the tables chosen for the query. It is best if these relationships have been created in the relationships window. However, temporary relationships can be created in the query design window by dragging a field from one table to another.

To add all the tables in the **Total Health and Fitness** database to a query:

1 Starting at the database window, click on the **QUERY** tab and click on **NEW**. Select **DESIGN VIEW** and click on **OK**.

2 From the **SHOW TABLE** dialog box, add all the tables. These are **Client**, **Client Status**, **Reservation**, and **Session**.

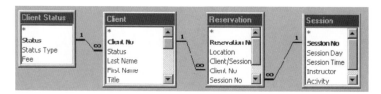

3 If there are no relationship lines or some missing, abandon the query and check the relationships using **TOOLS – RELATIONSHIPS**. Refer back to Topic 22.

4 Remove the **Client Status** table from the query design. Consider why is it dangerous to delete the **Reservation** table.

5 Close the query without saving it.

If tables are added to a query and there is no relationship defined between them, Access may try to link them and this could be a time-consuming and unproductive process.

Joins between tables

Before you can use joins between tables, you must know the contents of the fields of the tables and which fields are related by common values. Assigning identical names to fields in different tables that contain related data is a common practice. This has been adhered to in the **Total Health and Fitness** database (for example, **Client No,** which is the link between the **Client** and **Reservation** tables).

Knowing the contents of your tables will help when you need to add tables to a query so that you add the tables containing the data you wish to access and also any additional tables that are necessary to create links between the tables. This is discussed in more detail at the beginning of each multiple table query used in this topic.

In Access query design view, joins are indicated by lines linking field names in different tables.

Only one type of join, the inner-join, is used in our database application. Access allows other types of joins but this is the simplest. An inner-join will display all the records in one table that have corresponding records in another table. This correspondence is determined by identical values in the fields that join the tables. In the case of the **Total Health and Fitness** database, all joins are based on a unique primary key field in one table and a field in the other table in a one-to-many relationship.

119

Adding tables to a query

From query design view this is simply a matter of selecting more than one table from the **SHOW TABLE** dialog box. Tables are shown in the query window with lines between them indicating the relationships. If you omit a table, choose **QUERY – SHOW TABLE** to display the **SHOW TABLE** dialog box again.

Deleting tables from a query

In query design view click on the title bar of the particular table and pressing the **DELETE** key. However, check the table was not providing an indirect link between two tables and also make any amendments to the query.

Using multiple tables

This section comprises a series of tasks in which questions are asked of the database and queries containing multiple tables are devised in order to answer the question posed.

Client fees

Q.   How much fee money has been collected from clients in the last six months?

A.   First decide which tables are needed. The data needed are the clients who have
renewed their clientship in the last six months, their status and the amount of the
fee. This data can be found in the **Client** table and the **Client Status** table. Is there
a link between these two tables? Yes, between **Status No** (primary key **Client
Status** table) and **Status No** (**Client** table), so only these two tables will be
required.

Before continuing, you should review the dates of renewal in the **Client** table and, if
necessary, update them so that several clients will be selected by this query.

To create the query:

1 From the database window select, the **QUERIES** object type and click on **NEW**.
Select **DESIGN VIEW**.

2 From the **SHOW TABLE** dialog box, select the **Client** table and the **Client
Status** table. These two tables should be shown in the query window with a link
between them.

3 Add the fields **Client No** and **Fee** to the query.

4 Create a calculated field that works out the length of time between the date of
last renewal and today's date. In the first field cell enter the expression:

Renewed: DateDiff("d",[Date of last renewal],Date())

This calculates the number of days from the date of the last renewal to today.

5 Run this query to see the result.

6 Return to the query design. Add the criteria **<182** (you may need to check your
records to see if this query will work) to find those with renewal dates less than
six months old.

7 Run this query to check and then return to design mode.

8 Click on the **TOTALS** button to create totals.

9 In the **Renewed** field select **WHERE** in the total cell and hide this field. In the
Client No field select **COUNT** and in the **Fee** field select **SUM**.

10 Run the query. The result should be the numbers of clients who have renewed
their membership in the last six months and the total of fees paid.

11 Save the query as **Recent fees paid**.

To create the report:

12 From the database window select the **REPORTS** object type and click on
NEW.

13 In the **NEW REPORT** dialog box, select the query **Recent fees paid** and use
AUTOREPORT: TABULAR to design a report.

14 Switch to Design view and edit the labels so your report is similar to the one
below. Save the report as **Recent fees paid**.

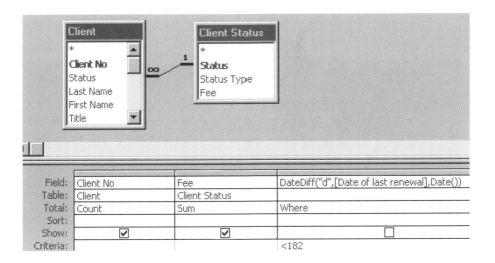

Field:	Client No	Fee	DateDiff("d",[Date of last renewal],Date())
Table:	Client	Client Status	
Total:	Count	Sum	Where
Sort:			
Show:	☑	☑	☐
Criteria:			<182

Fee receipts during last six months

No of clients renewing/joining	*Total fees paid*
6	£1,950.00

Sessions in a particular location

Q. What sessions are being held in the multi-gym?

A. The tables needed to answer this question are the **Reservation** table and the **Session** table. There is a direct link between these tables through **Session No**.

To create the query:

1 From the database window, select the **QUERIES** object type and click on **NEW**. Select Design view.

2 From the **SHOW TABLE** dialog box, select the **Session** table and the **Reservation** table. These two tables should be shown in the query window with a link between them.

3 Add the fields **Client/Session**, **Location**, **Session Day**, **Date**, **Time** and **Activity** to the query.

4 In the **Client/Session** column, set the criterion to **NO** to select sessions only and hide this field.

5 In **Location** put ***"Multi-gym"*** in the criteria row and hide this field.

6 Run the query.

7 Save this query as **Sessions in the Multi-gym**.

To create the report:

8 From the database window, select the **REPORTS** object type and click on **NEW**.

9 In the **NEW REPORT** dialog box, select the query **Sessions in the Multi-gym** and use **AUTOREPORT: TABULAR** to design a report.

10 Edit your design to create a report similar to the one below. Save this report as **Multi-gym sessions**.

Session activities in the Multi-gym

Day	Date	Time	Activity
1 Monday	8/5/00	15:00	Group Exercise
2 Tuesday	9/5/00	10:00	Sport performance
2 Tuesday	9/5/00	19:00	Fit Kids
3 Wednesday	10/5/00	19:00	Group exercise
4 Thursday	11/5/00	11:00	Weight management
4 Thursday	11/5/00	15:00	Sport performance
5 Friday	12/5/00	14:00	Sport performance
6 Saturday	13/5/00	14:00	Fit Kids
6 Saturday	13/5/00	15:00	Weight management

Session attendance

Q.   Which clients are attending which sessions?

A.   Our database is unable to answer this question. Why? The data needed has not been recorded. The database could be modified so this data can be added. What would be the best way to go about this? One method could be to introduce an extra field, class, which is added to the **Client** table. However, this leads to problems if the client attends more than one class or a class is cancelled. A better alternative is to create another table that keeps lists of clients in sessions. This table would be linked to both the **Client** table and the **Session** table. **Session List** would be a suitable name for this table.

To create the **Session List** table:

1 From the database window, select the **TABLES** object type and click on **NEW**. Select **DESIGN VIEW** and click on **OK**.

2 Create a table with two fields, **Session No** and **Client No**. Make both fields numeric of type long integer. This is so that they are of a type which will correspond to the AutoNumber types used by the fields **Client No** (**Client** table) and **Session No** (**Session** table) to which they will be related.

3 Each record is unique – that is, the entire record is not a field on its own. Therefore, the primary key must be both fields. To set both as the primary key, select both before clicking on the **PRIMARY KEY** button on the toolbar.

4 Define two relationships as described below. In both these relationships, referential integrity is enforced. This will prevent a session or client number being entered that does not exist in the **Session** or **Client** table, so a non-existent client cannot join a session nor can a client join a non-existent session.

5 Click on the **RELATIONSHIPS** button and then click on the **SHOW TABLE** button. Add the **Session List** table.

6 Drag **Session No** from the **Session** table to **Session No** in the **Session List** table. Check the **ENFORCE REFERENTIAL INTEGRITY** check box.

7 Drag **Client No** from the **Client** table to **Client No** in the **Session List** table. Check the **ENFORCE REFERENTIAL INTEGRITY** check box.

8 Save the layout and close the **RELATIONSHIPS** window.

Before a form can be created, first a query which links the client's name to the class activity needs to be created. A form can be created from this query to list the names of clients in each class.

9 From the database window, select the **QUERIES** object type and click on **NEW**. Select **DESIGN VIEW** and click on **OK**.

10 From the **ADD TABLE** dialog box, select the **Session List** table and the **Client** table. These three tables should be shown in the query window with links between them.

11 Add the following fields to the query: **Session No**, **Activity**, **Client No**, **First Name** and **Last Name**. Save the query as **Session Client List**. Close the query.

12 From the database window, select the **FORMS** object type and click on **NEW**. In the **NEW FORM** dialog box, select the **Session Client List** query just created and use the **AUTOFORM: TABULAR** to create a tabular form.

13 Add a title to the form and save the form as **Session Client List**.

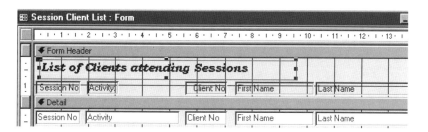

Exporting, importing and creating web pages

Topic objectives

Data can be exported from Access tables to text files, spreadsheets and to other database formats. Data can be imported from other database formats, spreadsheets and tabulated text.

An alternative is to make data available to others via the Internet, and Access provides a Wizard to enable you to do this.

This topic will show you how to:

- export and import between Access databases
- export a table to a text file
- export a table to a spreadsheet or alternative database format
- create web pages.

Exporting to another Access database

1 First create a blank database called **THF Copy**. Close that database and open the **Total Health and Fitness** database. To export the **Client Status** table and its data to the new database select the Client table in the database window.

2 Choose **FILE – EXPORT**.

3 In the **EXPORT TABLE 'CLIENT STATUS' TO**... dialog box, choose the folder in which you have saved the new database. Highlight the **THF Copy** database and click on **SAVE**.

4 In the **EXPORT** dialog box you can choose whether to keep the table name or rename it for the new database. Keep the table name **Status**. Choose the option **DEFINITION AND DATA** in the **EXPORT** section and click on **OK**.

5 Close **Total Health and Fitness** and open the **THF Copy** database and inspect the table just exported.

6 Close this database and open **Total Health and Fitness** and export the **Client** table to the **THF Copy** database but this time choose **DEFINITION ONLY**.

7 You can export other database objects to this database. Try exporting the **Client** form to the **THF Copy** database. Note that as both databases are Access 2000, this is feasible but, if you want to export to earlier versions of Access, you can export tables only.

Importing Access data from another Access database

Database objects can be transferred between Access 2000 databases, either by importing or exporting. We have considered exporting as this is a good way to set up a new database that has a lot of the features of your current one. Importing is a useful way to copy objects from an existing database into your current database. The steps involved in importing will be described here, but this does not constitute an actual exercise.

To import a table or other database object:

Choose **FILE – GET EXTERNAL DATA – IMPORT** then select the folder in which the database you wish to import from is located. Select the database and click on the **IMPORT** button.

Tick items listed to select them, and select the different tabs for different database objects. If you click on the options button you can choose various import settings such as definition only for tables.

Note: After importing or exporting an object, it is in both databases and there is no link between the two copies of the object. So, for example, if the object is updated in one database it will not be updated in another.

Exporting a table to a text file

125

It may often be appropriate to select a set of records from a table and export them to a word processor for further formatting or for integration into a text-based document.

To export the **Session** table to a text file:

1 Select the **TABLES** object type and highlight the **Session** table.

2 Choose **FILE – EXPORT**. In the **EXPORT** ... dialog box, choose the folder in which you wish to save the file. Save it in the same folder as your database is in.

3 Select the rich text file type from the **SAVE AS TYPE** list box and accept the filename suggested **Session**. Click on **SAVE**.

4 View the file **SESSION.RTF** using Word or other word processor.

Exporting a table to a spreadsheet

To export the **Session** table to a spreadsheet file:

1 Open the database containing the table you wish to export and select the table.

2 Choose **FILE – EXPORT**. In the **EXPORT** ... dialog, choose the folder in which you wish to save the file. Save it in the same folder as your database is in.

3 Select the Excel 97-2000 type from the **SAVE AS TYPE** list box and accept the filename suggested **Session**. Click on **SAVE**.

4 View the file **SESSION.XLS** using Excel.

Note: As well as tables, you can easily export queries in text or spreadsheet form. You can also select data in tables and queries and copy it into a word-processed document or spreadsheet.

Publishing a database on the World Wide Web

Some or all the data in a database may be information that could be made available to clients on the World Wide Web. For instance, clients could check and make reservations.

In order to utilise the Internet properly, you need to post your database and its associated web pages on your web server. Access provides Wizards to help you create web pages. There are three types of web page you can create:

- Static HTML files. These can be created from tables, queries, forms and reports. Once created, these files are no longer part of the database and are really for an information-only purpose. For example, the **Session** table could be converted to HTML and used in this way.
- Data-access pages. These are connected to the database allowing data to be entered and edited over the Internet. This is more complex as issues regarding security on your web site would need to be resolved (e.g. bona fide clients only could make reservations). This extra detail is outside the scope of this book.
- Server-generated HTML files. These are outside the scope of this book.

To create a static HTML file from the **Session** report:

1 Select the **REPORTS** object type and highlight the **Session** report.

2 Choose **FILE – EXPORT**. In the **EXPORT . . .** dialog box, choose the folder in which you wish to save the file. Save it in the same folder as your database is in.

3 Select the HTML type from the **SAVE AS TYPE** list box and accept the filename suggested **Session**. Click on **SAVE**.

4 View the file **SESSION.HTML** using your browser. If you have an HTML editor and are familiar with its use, you may wish to add links and make formatting changes. This file could be uploaded to your server. Any changes to the schedule would require a new page being created and uploaded to replace the old one.

We will briefly consider creating a data access page, which will be saved under the **PAGES** object type and can be used locally as an illustration of how these pages work.

1 Select the **PAGES** object type. Double-click on **CREATE DATA ACCESS PAGE BY USING WIZARD**.

2 Select **Reservation** in the **TABLES/QUERIES** drop-down list. Add all the fields to the page by clicking on `>>`. Click on **NEXT>**.

3 If any grouping has been selected, click on `<` to remove it since we wish to have read/write access to this page. Click on **NEXT>**.

4 Choose to sort the records in **Date** and then **Time** order. Click on **NEXT>**.

5 Accept the title *Reservation* and click on **FINISH**.

6 You are shown your page in Design view and, if you wish, you can adjust the positions of the controls. Save the form as **RESERVATION.HTM** in the same folder as your database is stored in.

7 View this web page with your browser and try making a new reservation and altering an existing one. If you wish this to work on the Internet, you should consult Access help and your service provider for more information.

Database application – switchboard forms

Topic objectives

A database application is a set of related database objects you can use to accomplish a particular task, such as managing the data for Total Health and Fitness. In such an application, certain forms and reports will be used frequently. A database application is designed to give easy access to those forms and reports through an easy-to-use interface.

A switchboard form provides this database application interface. It is a special form that allows you to open forms and reports you have created from a central menu. The switchboard form has buttons you can click to open specified forms and reports. If your application has different areas such as customers, products and orders, you can have several switchboards, the first allowing you to choose the area to work in, which, in turn, opens other switchboards that open forms and reports that belong to that area.

This topic will show you how to:

- create a switchboard form
- edit a switchboard form
- create additional switchboard pages.

Creating and managing a switchboard form

If you use the Database Wizard to create a database, Access automatically creates a switchboard form that helps you to navigate around the database. If you want to create a switchboard for a database you have created yourself, use the Switchboard Manager.

To create a switchboard form by using the Switchboard Manager:

1. Choose **TOOLS – DATABASE UTILITIES** and select **SWITCHBOARD MANAGER**.

2. If you have not created a switchboard, Access will ask you if you would like to create a switchboard. Choose **YES**.

3. In the **SWITCHBOARD MANAGER** dialog box, click on the **EDIT** button. In the **EDIT SWITCHBOARD PAGE** dialog box, key in the name *Main Menu*, for the switchboard in the switchboard name box, and then click **NEW**.

4. In the **EDIT SWITCHBOARD ITEM** dialog box, key in the text, *New Client*, for the first switchboard button in the **TEXT** box. Open the Command box and select **OPEN FORM IN ADD MODE**, and, in the **FORM** box, select the form **Client**. Click on **OK**.

5 Steps 3 and 4 are repeated for all the items to be added to the switchboard. Click on **NEW** to add another menu item, this time **TEXT – AMEND CLIENT DETAILS, COMMAND – OPEN FORM IN EDIT MODE, FORM – CLIENT**2.

6 If you want to edit or delete an item, click the item in the **ITEMS ON THIS SWITCHBOARD** box, and then click **EDIT** or **DELETE**. If you want to rearrange items, click the item in the box and then click **MOVE UP** or **MOVE DOWN**.

7 Add a **CLOSE** item by choosing **TEXT – CLOSE, COMMAND – EXIT APPLICATION**. Click on **CLOSE** in Edit Switchboard Page and **CLOSE** in the Switchboard Manager dialog box.

8 Open the switchboard form and test the function of buttons the Switchboard Manager has programmed (Figure 25.1). Although it is best to leave the design of this form as it is (because you could stop it from working), you can edit layout, colours, text and font on the form by switching to design view.

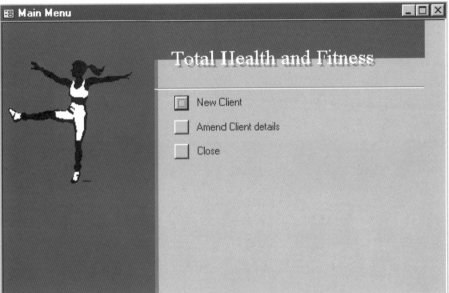

FIGURE 25.1

129

Note: Depending on which command you click, Access displays another box below the command box. Click an item in this box, if necessary. For example, if you clicked **OPEN FORM IN EDIT MODE** in the command box, click the name of the form you want to open in the **FORM** box, such as **AMEND PRODUCT** details, and then click **OK**.

When you create a switchboard with the Switchboard Manager, Access creates a **SWITCHBOARD ITEMS** table that describes what the buttons on the form display. Don't make any changes to this table as you may stop the switchboard form from working properly.

Creating a multi-page switchboard

You can use the Switchboard Manager to create a switchboard that has buttons to open other switchboard pages. This allows you to group different functions on different pages, thereby improving the user interface with the database.

1. Choose **TOOLS – DATABASE UTILITIES**, and select **SWITCHBOARD MANAGER**. Click on **NEW** and enter *Client management for the name of this switchboard page*. Select this page and click on **EDIT**.

2. Add two items *New Client* and *Amend Client details* as described previously. Add a **Main Menu** item with the command **GO TO SWITCHBOARD** and choose the Main Menu switchboard. Close the **Client management** switchboard page.

3. Select the Main Menu page and choose **EDIT**. Delete the New Client and Amend Client Details items previously created as they are now on the client management page.

4. Add another item Client management with the command Go to switchboard and choose **CLIENT MANAGEMENT**. Use the **MOVE UP** button to put this above the Close item. Close the switchboard and try it out.

5. Return to the switchboard manager and add a **Session management** page that has the items, **New Session**, **Session booking** and **Main menu**. Add a Session Management command (Figure 25.2) to the Main menu page to open the session management page.

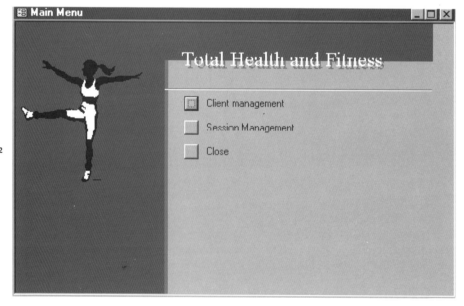

FIGURE 25.2

Editing a switchboard

When the switchboard is being modified as it is being developed, it has a command 'Design Application' that will take you straight into the Switchboard Manager:

1. Open the Switchboard Manager and choose **MAIN MENU** from the switchboard pages list and click on **EDIT**. Add a Modify switchboard item with

a Design application command.

 Use the **MOVE UP** button to move this item above Close. Close the Switchboard Manager and try out the switchboard form.

Note: Items on switchboard pages can be removed using the **DELETE** button in the **EDIT SWITCHBOARD PAGE** dialog box. Switchboard pages can be removed using the **DELETE** button in the **SWITCHBOARD MANAGER** dialog box.

The switchboard page that is marked as default will be the page displayed when the form is opened. To make a switchboard page the one that is opened when you open the form, select the switchboard name in the **SWITCHBOARD MANAGER** dialog box and click on the **MAKE DEFAULT** button.

Improving the switchboard

To add a reports page that will give you a menu of different reports, first create another switchboard page called **Reports** and add the following items:

- *Client report* , which use the **OPEN REPORT** command to open the **Client** report.
- *Client fees* , which opens the **Recent fees paid** report.
- *Sessions* , which opens the **Session** report
- *Main Menu* which opens the **Main Menu** switchboard page.

Add another item *Reports to* the **Main Menu** page that opens the *Reports* switchboard page.

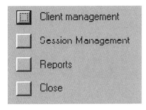

Items on Main Menu page   Items on Reports page

As the **Total Health and Fitness** database application develops and further forms and reports are created, commands to open these can be added to the switchboard form. If you find you are adding too many items to a page, split the page into two by creating another page. Try to think how the database is to be used and exploit the user-friendly potential of the switchboard.

APPENDIX

Client table data

Client No	Status	Last Name	First Name	Title	Street	Town	County	Post Code	Telephone No	Profession	Date of Birth	Date of Joining	Date of Last Renewal	Fitness Interests	Smoker	Gender
1	2	Roche	Paul J	Mr	32 The Beeches	Harrogate	Yorkshire	YO2 6TR	01432 569236	Marketing Manager	3/12/65	10/2/98	10/2/00	Sport performance, squash, swimming	✓	✓
2	3	Price	Hilary	Mrs	29 Ripon Drive	Knaresborough	Yorkshire	YO7 8YU	01432 552099	Lawyer	29/11/60	6/10/98	6/10/99	Yoga, aqua aerobics		✓
3	4	Price	Jason R	Mr	29 Ripon Drive	Knaresborough	Yorkshire	YO7 8YU			6/3/88	6/10/98	6/10/99	Karate		✓
4	1	Williams	Ann M	Miss	4 Smithy Grove	Harrogate	Yorkshire	YO3 5TY	01432 569945	Beauty consultant	5/8/73	2/12/98	2/12/99	Aqua aerobics		
5	1	Woodall	Daniel	Mr	1 Hornby Drive	Harrogate	Yorkshire	YO2 6DY		Sales Executive	4/12/70	16/1/99	16/1/99	Body pump, judo	✓	✓
6	6	Harris	Pamela	Mrs	35 Oakdene Court	Spofforth	Yorkshire	YO11 2DZ	01435 890523	Personal Assistant	7/7/74	2/2/99	2/2/00			
7	5	Harris	Peter G	Mr	35 Oakdene Court	Spofforth	Yorkshire	YO11 2DZ	01432 569311	Buyer	22/8/70	2/2/99	2/2/00	Sport performance, body pump	✓	✓
8	2	Mirze	Ivan	Mr	17 Jubilee Gardens	Harrogate	Yorkshire	YO1 2GV	01432 561553	Accountant	15/3/55	15/4/99	15/4/00	Sub aqua, sport performance		✓
9	1	Johnson	Janet E	Mrs	42 Tabley Road	Knaresborough	Yorkshire	YO7 3DR	01432 557822	Business Analyst	10/3/63	5/5/99	5/5/00	Personal Fitness, Aqua aerobics		
10	1	Kelly	John D	Mr	61 St Marys Road	Harrogate	Yorkshire	YO1 5LR		Engineer	10/2/58	22/5/99	22/5/99	Sport performance		✓
11	6	Lo	Dennis	Mr	56 Underwood Lane	Harrogate	Yorkshire	YO4 6WN	01432 569066	Restaurant Owner	14/7/77	14/6/99	14/6/99			✓
12	5	Grant	Frances	Ms	3 Coleridge Way	Knaresborough	Yorkshire	YO7 5TR	01435 894471	Headteacher	25/10/51	30/6/99	30/6/99	Low impact aerobics	✓	✓
13	5	Butler	William	Mr	6 Park Road	Harrogate	Yorkshire	YO1 3RE	01432 565715	Managing Director	12/4/47	23/7/99	23/7/99	Judo, body pump	✓	✓
14	5	McKay	Caroline	Miss	19 Cloverfields	Harrogate	Yorkshire	YO2 4DA	01432 567351	Deputy Headteacher		5/8/99	5/8/99	Yoga		
15	1	Corbett	George	Mr	6 The Square	Knaresborough	Yorkshire	YO7 1YJ	01432 551431	Director	1/2/65	22/8/99	22/8/99	Aerobics, squash, swimming	✓	✓
16	3	Anderson	Christopher	Mr	19 Moss Street	Harrogate	Yorkshire	YO2 7ER	01432 568812	Chief Inspector	18/5/58	10/9/99	10/9/99	Body pump		✓
17	3	Anderson	Amanda	Mrs	19 Moss Street	Harrogate	Yorkshire	YO2 7ER	01432 568812	Housewife	30/7/62	10/9/99	10/9/99	High impact aerobics, yoga		✓
18	4	Anderson	Lionel	Mr	19 Moss Street	Harrogate	Yorkshire	YO2 7ER	01432 568812		30/12/87	10/9/99	10/9/99	Fit Kids		✓
19	4	Anderson	Zara	Miss	19 Moss Street	Harrogate	Yorkshire	YO2 7ER	01432 568812		10/2/89	10/9/99	10/9/99	Fit Kids		✓
20	1	Evans	Anthony J	Mr	74 Platt Avenue	Harrogate	Yorkshire	YO2 3TF	01432 567333	Transport Manager	22/12/58	1/11/99	1/11/99	Body Pump	✓	✓

Client Status table data

Status	Status Type	Fee
1	Adult Gold	£400.00
2	Adult Silver	£350.00
3	Adult Family	£250.00
4	Child Family	£100.00
5	Business	£300.00
6	Social	£150.00

Session table data

Session No	Session Day	Session Time	Instructor	Activity	Gender Mix
1	1	10:00	Joy	Aqua Aerobics	Female
2	1	19:00	Andy	Body Pump	Male
3	1	15:00	Rob	Group Exercise	Mixed
4	1	19:00	Diane	Low Impact Aerobics	Mixed
5	2	10:00	Andy	Sport Performance	Male
6	2	14:00	Diane	High Impact Aerobics	Female
7	2	19:00	Peter	Fit Kids	Mixed
8	3	15:00	Joy	Aqua Aerobics	Female
9	3	20:00	Andy	Body pump	Mixed
10	3	19:00	Fran	Yoga	Female
11	3	19:00	Rob	Group Exercise	Mixed
12	4	11:00	Joy	Weight Management	Female
13	4	14:00	Diane	Low Impact Aerobics	Mixed
14	4	15:00	Andy	Sport Performance	Female
15	4	19:00	Lionel	Body Spinning	Mixed
16	5	10:00	Fran	Yoga	Female
17	5	11:00	Diane	High Impact Aerobics	Mixed
18	5	14:00	Dave	Sport Performance	Male
26	6	14:00	Barry	Fit Kids	Mixed
27	6	15:00	Carol	Weight Management	Female
28	6	11:00	Sharon	Aqua Aerobics	Mixed
29	7	11:00	Trevor	Body pump	Male
30	7	11:00	Barry	Fit Kids	Mixed

133

Reservation table data

Reservation No	Location	Client/Session	Client No	Session No	Date	Time
1	Pool			1	8/5/00	10:00
2	Fitness Floor			2	8/5/00	19:00
3	Multi-gym			3	8/5/00	15:00
4	Fitness Floor			4	8/5/00	19:00
5	Multi-gym			5	9/5/00	10:00
6	Fitness Floor			6	9/5/00	14:00
7	Multi-gym			7	9/5/00	19:00
8	Pool			8	10/5/00	15:00
9	Fitness Floor			9	10/5/00	20:00
10	Fitness Floor			10	10/5/00	19:00
11	Multi-gym			11	10/5/00	19:00
12	Multi-gym			12	11/5/00	11:00
13	Fitness Floor			13	11/5/00	14:00
14	Multi-gym			14	11/5/00	15:00
15	Cycle Room			15	11/5/00	19:00
16	Fitness Floor			16	12/5/00	10:00
17	Fitness Floor			17	12/5/00	11:00
18	Multi-gym			18	12/5/00	14:00
19	Pool	✓	16		13/5/00	18:00
20	Fitness Floor	✓	5		13/5/00	14:00
21	Fitness Floor	✓	15		14/5/00	15:00
22	Pool	✓	2		14/5/00	19:00
23	Multi-gym			26	13/5/00	14:00
24	Multi-gym			27	13/5/00	15:00
25	Pool			28	13/5/00	11:00
26	Fitness Floor			29	14/5/00	11:00
27	Multi-gym			30	14/5/00	11:00

Session List table data

Session No	Client No
1	2
1	5
1	16
4	4
4	7
5	7
5	10
9	1
9	8
9	12
10	2
10	5
10	16

INDEX